If You Can't Say NO

You Can't *Really* Say YES

Reclaiming Your Personal Power to Choose

C. Jefferson Hood, Ph.D.

P.O. Box 110302
Nashville, TN 37222

© Copyright. 1996. C. Jefferson Hood. All rights reserved.

ISBN: 0-9654062-0-2

Typography and design by JM Productions, Brentwood, TN 37024-1911

Cover design: Ron Watson

CONTENTS

Introduction vii

PART ONE: LEARNING THE BASICS

1. The Power of Choice 3
   You Always Have a Choice
2. Managing the Reserve Tank 13
   Discovering Your Power to Choose
3. Just Say "No!" 27
   Exploring the Vital Role of Boundaries
4. Speaking Up In Relationships 49
   Reclaiming Your Power to Choose with Loved Ones
5. We Need to Talk! 57
   Communicating What You Need to Others

PART TWO: CHALLENGING OLD MESSAGES

6. Can You Feel Anything When I Do This? 71
   Reconnecting With Your Emotions
7. Cooling the Volcano 85
   Expressing Anger in a Healthy Manner
8. Carefully Following Poor Maps 95
   How the Script You Follow Can Affect Your Choices
9. "Sugar and Spice and Everything Nice" 107
   Crippling Elements of Women's Roles
10. What's a "Real Man" Anyway? 121
    Creating a New Map for Masculinity
11. There's No Such Thing as "Had To!" 131
    Generating Alternative Choices

PART THREE: HEALING THE WOUNDS

12. Plugging the Leaks 143
    Healing the Reserve Tank
13. Something Terrible Happened 153
    Dealing With the Pain of Abuse

14. Hoarding Worthless Stones.................. 163
    Understanding Forgiveness

PART FOUR: FACING SPECIAL CHALLENGES

15. Sex is More Than Body Parts............... 177
    Developing a Healthy Sexuality
16. What's Wrong With Us?.................... 191
    Problem-Solving When Relationships Don't Improve
17. I Gave at the Office....................... 201
    Balancing Work With the Rest of Life
18. What's God Got to Do With It? 211
    Spirituality and Choices

DEDICATION

THIS BOOK IS DEDICATED to Linda: my wife, my friend, my lover. I'm fortunate that on an August afternoon you made me your choice. Thank you for your unqualified support.

INTRODUCTION

If YOU CAN'T SAY NO, YOU CAN'T REALLY SAY YES.
If you believe you can't turn someone down, that you have no choice but to say yes, you'll feel trapped. If you think that there's only one option available to you, you'll tend to be resentful. Only when you see that you have the freedom of choice—the freedom to choose from among many choices—can you truly enjoy life. Only when you're convinced that you have the freedom to say no, only then can you truly say yes to the questions, challenges and opportunities life presents.

Men and women who believe they have no choices will be miserable. You'll feel limited. You'll often feel empty or burned out. You may perceive yourself as being a pawn that's pushed about by other, more powerful players. Life will seem to offer no handles with which you can lift, move or direct your existence. Restoring your ability to choose is a key element to getting more fulfillment out of life.

Others may appear to be getting what they want while you don't. When you observe the people around you, you may conclude that most of them are able to control their worlds. It's only you who is being manipulated by circumstances. It's not true. My experience is that all of us have given away some of our choices. Many of you have given away most of your choices.

You don't have to live like this! The premise of this book is simple: you can reclaim your power of choice and live a fuller life. The only way you can be truly satisfied with your life is to experience fully your *personal power to choose*. If you've lost your sense of choice, you'll feel manipulated, coerced and controlled. When you can regain your power of choice, you'll get more out of life and have more life in your life.

Are you ready to get more out of life? Then come along. Choose to choose!

PART ONE

LEARNING THE BASICS

1

THE POWER OF CHOICE
You Always Have a Choice

SEVERAL YEARS ago when *Keith and his wife, Amanda, married, they found a beautiful, two-story, four-bedroom house which they wanted to purchase. They applied for the loan and made their offer on the house. They were approved for the mortgage and the sellers accepted the price on the house that they'd offered. They were excited to be able to acquire such a home.

Two days before they were to close, the loan officer called Keith with some news that needed immediate attention. His supervisor had gone over their financial records again and said that the percentages weren't right. The bottom line was that in order to qualify for the loan, they'd need to eliminate at least two hundred dollars a month in debt. Keith expressed his frustration with him for not catching this sooner. The loan officer listened, but there was no way to bend the rules at the mortgage company to accommodate them without lowering their debt ratio.

Keith and Amanda discussed what to do and made a decision to sell the car he was driving. That would lower their monthly expense more than enough for them to qualify for their loan. Within 24 hours they'd sold the car, closed on their loan and moved into that new house. They found an older model car which they purchased with cash. Keith drove that car for the next three years.

Here's the question I'd like for you to consider: Did they "have to" sell Keith's car? That's certainly one way they could have looked at it. "I had to sell my late model Chevy!" They could have been angry and resentful about it. Every time he turned into his driveway,

---

*All the examples and illustrations in this book grew out of my clinical practice and speaking experience, but the names and details have been altered in order to protect the identity of those whose accounts I've chosen to share.

Keith could have remembered the inconvenience they'd suffered in order to qualify for the loan.

Instead, they looked at things differently. On the infrequent occasions when they thought about it at all, Keith and Amanda thought, "We chose to sell that car in order to qualify for the loan on our beautiful home." As far as they were concerned, that's really what had happened. They'd made a *choice*. They didn't have to sell the car; they only needed to sell it if they wanted to purchase this house. It was a trade off. In a world full of choices, Keith and Amanda chose to take a step back in one part of their lives (the quality of their automobiles) in order to enhance another area of their lives (the size and style of home they lived in). They didn't "have to." They made this choice in order to get something in return.

Keith could have continued to drive that shiny, maroon car if he'd wanted to do so. They would have needed to buy a less expensive house or continued to rent a much smaller place, but they could have done it. To them the choices were clear—keep the car that could be replaced with something much cheaper *or* keep the house they'd found that had so much potential. They could hang on to a car that was already three years old and would steadily depreciate in value or buy a house that they were getting below market value at a time when property values were steadily rising. In the end it turned out to be a very good decision. Three years later Keith had another car and the house they'd bought had increased in value by thirty-five percent!

Choices! You're all making choices. Business choices. Housing choices. Spiritual choices. Relationship choices. Emotional choices. Recreational choices. Health-related choices. Sexual choices. Every day is filled with choices. You're living right now with the results of the myriad of choices you've made.

The Sad Life of Forgotten Choices

It's difficult to live with the results of relinquished choices. The quality of life of those who regularly give away their choices is consistently lower than the satisfaction enjoyed by those who exercise their power to choose. Sandy had been involved emotionally and sexually with Edwin for almost six years. They'd met at work. Their relationship had started as a casual friendship, then grown deeper as they shared emotionally. They'd been sexually involved for over five years. Edwin said he loved her. He said he wanted to be with her. He assured Sandy that he wanted a life with her. Because she cared so

The Power of Choice

much for him, she'd been willing to wait while Edwin went through his divorce.

The problem which brought her to counseling was that while Edwin was unhappily married, and had been unhappily married for 17 years, he couldn't seem to take action toward getting the divorce he told Sandy he wanted. He'd assured her when they met that he was separated from his wife and was getting a divorce, but six years later he was no closer to filing than he'd been the day they met. Sandy began to put pressure on Edwin to make a decision. She was exhausted with his promises; she'd lived her life in limbo for as long as she cared to do so. She told him that she loved him, but didn't choose to continue to wait on him unless he took the actions which he'd promised he would.

Sandy asked Edwin to talk to the counselor and when he arrived, he appeared confused and tired. He sat stiffly on the couch in the counselor's office. He wore his $900 suit and his $400 shoes as symbols which proclaimed he had it all together, but as he talked it was clear he didn't feel that way. His life was a mess and as he told his story, his pain and sadness were evident.

Edwin explained to the therapist why he couldn't make a choice. He was painfully torn between this woman he said he loved and his sense of duty to his children. He said without hesitation that he cared nothing for his wife and had lived apart from her for the last seven years. A job transfer had made it convenient for him to move away from his hometown. He traveled home to visit his children most every weekend and relished the time he had with them. While he said he had no desire to make things work with his wife, he couldn't stand the thought of giving up any of the time he spent with his children when he traveled home on weekends. He was afraid that a divorce would limit that time.

He was depressed, he said, because he couldn't decide what to do. He wanted to be with Sandy, but he couldn't bring himself to be away from his children any more than he was already. He feared that a divorce would weaken an already faltering relationship with his sons. He felt stuck.

As he wrestled with this decision, the pressure to perform at work was being increased. His company was reorganizing, down-sizing to cut expenses. He had more to do and less support from subordinates because so many had been outplaced. He felt as though he were being squeezed in the twin jaws of a large and powerful vice.

Although Edwin said he couldn't decide, in truth he really had. As was his pattern in this and other parts of his life, he didn't make decisions until the moment just before the final deadline was reached. In fact, if he could get someone else to make the decision, he wouldn't actively make a choice at all. The truth was, his habit of making decisions by default was still decision making, but the people around him resented his style and he didn't experience any sense of his own *personal power to choose.*

All the while, he complained of the demands others were putting on him. He was angry at the limitations his relationships seemed to be putting on his life.

"Blast my wife for threatening to take the boys away from me!"

"How can Sandy put such pressure on me when she knows how hard I'm trying?"

"My boss expects too much from me. How can I handle all these work responsibilities?"

What he needed to do in order to feel more powerful was to reclaim his choices. This was the one thing he didn't seem ready to do. Edwin felt impotent, as if everyone else were running his life. In the end, it was Sandy who broke off their relationship when he continued to balk at making a commitment to her. He'd given away his choices for so long, he couldn't see any way to take responsibility. Sadly, his therapy ended because he wasn't ready to take responsibility for his life. He continued to say, "I don't have any choice."

You Can Choose!

This is a book about choices. It's about the choices you see you have. It's about the choices you only wish you could have. It's about the choices which are yours even when you say, "I had no choice!"

The truth is you *always* have a choice! None of your choices may be very appealing. The best you can come up with might be your choice from among the least objectionable of several poor choices. But you still have choices. One choice may stand out as being easier, more tolerable, more diplomatic, less problematic, or more desirable, but that doesn't make it your only choice.

When you say, "I had no choice," at best you're saying that the other choices were for some reason so undesirable you picked this one. At worst, it means you chickened out or chose not to take a stand. Let me repeat: there are *always* choices.

The Power of Choice

Unless you're a child or in prison, no one is forcing you to do anything. For instance, I have talked with women who thought that they were trapped in an abusive relationship. For a time, maybe for a long time, they were so convinced that they were "caught" that they stayed in intolerable circumstances. They lived with the threat of or actually experienced emotional, verbal and/or physical abuse. Their fear and concern were very real to them.

Then something remarkable happened—they became strong enough to leave. They got out of their abusive relationships. With some it happened slowly; with others it was an instantaneous decision. However the decision was made, it was made. A new choice was exercised. They found shelters or support groups that could help. They involved their families. They called the police. They took out orders of protection and restraining orders. Some moved out of state. They became stronger and when they did so, they realized that they had choices that in the past had eluded them.

It's not my intent to minimize the difficulty of reclaiming your choices. It takes time, work, courage and retraining to regain your ***personal power to choose***. It will be painful and frightful to take back your power to vote in your own life. You may do what you need to do to change your life one small step at a time. But you can do it! You don't have to live with less than what you want.

We all have choices. If you're an adult, you're doing what you're doing for a living, you're living where you're living, and you're with the person you're with because you've chosen to do so!

A New Recipe

If you want more than you've been getting, you'll have to change what you've been doing. An old recipe won't lead to a new dish. Unless you do something differently, you'll get what you've gotten.

Suppose your Aunt Emma makes the best chocolate brownies you've ever tasted, and you ask her for her recipe. You take it home and prepare this tasty treat, expecting your efforts to turn out like hers. Instead, you make the brownies and they're a big flop. So you try again. And several more times. Every time the results are poor. How long would you continue to follow the same recipe, leading to unwanted results, before you said to yourself, "There's something wrong here! I've got to do something differently!" Maybe your aunt copied the recipe down incorrectly. Perhaps you're deciphering it improperly. Maybe you've been using some old baking powder or the wrong sort of flour. Perhaps your oven cooks at an inaccurate temperature. Whatever the explanation might be for your problem, you'll have to do something differently if you want to prepare those brownies that you've enjoyed so much when Aunt Emma cooked them.

One definition of insanity is to do what you've been doing expecting that somehow this time you'll get a different result. That kind of thinking is unproductive. In fact, it's downright crazy. Remember this—

*If you continue to do what you've always done,
you'll continue to get the same outcome.*

Consequences of Relinquished Choices

If you relinquish to others your power to make choices, you suffer in several ways. First, you fail to become responsible and experience the maturity that comes from making choices and experiencing the outcomes, good or bad. Like a child learning to walk, you need to know that if you lean too far this way or that way, you'll fall over. If someone else were always catching you when you were a pupil in the pedestrian arts, learning to walk would be an impossible task. The failures are part of the learning experience! A child learns to relish the success of being able to stand and walk without support. There's a sense of discipline and accomplishment which follows.

Edwin, the man who was wrestling with his choice to stay in his marriage or get out, hadn't cultivated this maturity. Instead, he would waiver back and forth from one day to the next, unable to take decisive steps in one direction or the other. Even though he held a responsible job and had achieved a high level of professional success, he felt little joy in life and almost no sense of satisfaction. He felt down and depressed, emotions he covered by staying busy at work.

Secondly, when you make decisions by default there's little sense that life has any handles; everything seems to be beyond your control. Fate, chance and luck seem to determine your fortune. Others appear to take advantage of you. When you fail to determine *what* you want, establish limits to get it, and back up these limits with conditions or consequences, you set yourself up to feel victimized. The only way out of this dissatisfying sort of life is to accept responsibility for setting clear boundaries and stand behind them.

Finally, when your decisions are made by others, you sense a powerlessness which empties your emotional reserve tank, the reservoir inside of you which holds your emotional energy. Control of your tank is turned over to others. You'll feel empty, tired, and burned out. The concept of the reserve tank is vital to your understanding of choices and will be discussed in great detail in the next chapter.

You can make your own choices. If you believe you can't do so, you'll be frustrated, feel used, and have a tremendous store of built up anger, tension, and anxiety. That list of energy-depleting emotions is an apt summary of the lives of many men and women. See if you're experiencing any of these emotions. If so, you've probably placed some or all of your choices in the hands of others.

Stop now and complete the following assessment. The results will be a helpful indicator of how well you're doing at taking charge of your choices.

CHOICE EXERCISE

- Do you harbor anger and resentment?
- Do you feel anxious most or all of the time?
- Do you often think someone is taking advantage of you?
- Do you find yourself complaining consistently about your job, your children, your family or your spouse?
- Does your conversational style sound whiny?
  - » "Can you believe she said that?"
  - » "Why can't I ever catch a break?"
  - » "Every time I turn around, something else bad is happening to me!"
- Are you tired a lot? Do you get an adequate amount of sleep only to find that you still wake up exhausted?
- Does it seem to be harder than it used to be for you to bounce back from a stressful day?
- Do you have a dream or dreams that you've never acted upon?

How did you do? If you marked only one or two, you're probably doing pretty well at experiencing your power to choose. If you marked three or more of these items, you're probably giving away too many of your choices.

Change Is Possible

Being able to choose isn't the same as being in control. You cannot control your world. Absolute control is a myth. Drive your car over an icy patch in the road and watch how quickly "control" can evaporate.

However, life doesn't just happen to you. You can speak in a clear and audible voice. You can set limits that enable you to get more of what you want and to receive less of what you don't want. The key is in recognizing and utilizing your *personal power to choose*.

Your life will seem to get crazy when you make one of two mistakes:

> *You fail to make choices in the areas where you do have personal power*
>
> **or**
>
> *You attempt to take control in areas where you have no personal power.*

Making either of these errors will rob you of some contentment. A lifetime of living these errors will lead to feelings of emptiness, burn-out and dissatisfaction.

The "Serenity Prayer" is a formal statement designed to help you avoid these two extremes. This beautiful prayer states, "God, grant me the serenity to accept the things I cannot change, courage to change the things I can, and the wisdom to know the difference." "The things I cannot change" are the areas of your world and your life over which you have no power. "The things I can" change are the areas where you can exercise your personal power. Healthy living results when you have the "wisdom" to see which things in your life are in which category and you respond accordingly.

There's good news and bad news. The good news is: you can get your choices back! The bad news is: it won't be easy! Simple, but not easy. In fact, the work that has to be done to regain your power to choose is so intense at times that some people have been frightened away. It takes hard work and great courage to undergo an intense inside look and do the hard work necessary to regain your choices. While it's extremely rewarding, this is some of the most difficult work you'll ever do. It's definitely not for the faint-hearted. Ever completely rebuilt an engine? Ever remodeled a house while you lived in it? Ever had the responsibility for revamping an entire system at work? Do you recall the time, energy and persistence those tasks required? The challenge to regain your choices will demand that much and more of you!

There's some encouraging news: You don't have to have a personality transplant in order to recognize and exercise your *personal power to choose*. There are skills to learn, clear boundaries to set, and a mind set to adopt which can change the course of your life. Change is possible!

Choose to explore this world of personal power. Dedicate yourself to regaining your power to choose.

POWER TO CHOOSE: Look back at your choice exercise on page 9. What do your answers say to you?

_____
_____
_____
_____
_____
_____
_____
_____

2
MANAGING THE RESERVE TANK
Discovering Your Power to Choose

HOWARD IS A FIFTY-YEAR-OLD EXECUTIVE who has experienced a great amount of career and financial success. He has a knack for investing in businesses which will make money. For years he was able to juggle a schedule that most other people would consider overwhelming as he made decisions which kept his eight to ten business interests running smoothly.

One day he began to realize that he couldn't bounce back from his tough days the way he used to. He felt tired all the time. His sleep was restless and he woke up fatigued.

Not coincidentally, his relationships with the important people in his life suffered. He was growing more distant from his teenage children and was constantly irritated by his wife. Lately, he said that he'd been unable to perform sexually. That was the final straw that brought him to therapy.

In describing himself and his mood, Howard used words like "tired," "empty," and "dead inside." He was burned out with his career. His sleep disturbance and his other symptoms suggested he was moderately depressed.

The Reserve Tank

Howard's depression was a sign that his reserve tank was nearing empty. Clients who come for therapy often use phrases like, "I'm feeling really low." Or they'll comment that they've "run out of gas." This sense of being empty is very real because each of us has an emotional reserve tank. The tank looks something like the illustration on page 14.

The level in your tank is an indication of the amount of emotional and behavioral energy you have available for meeting the challenges which life presents. If the level in your tank is low, you'll feel

If You Can't Say No You Can't Really Say Yes

Each of us has a reserve tank.

depleted, empty and tired. If your tank has a high level, you'll feel alive, vitalized and ready to meet the challenges of life.

Whether you're aware of the level in your tank or not, the present quantity of your emotional energy is affecting the way you feel and how you respond to the people and events in your world. If you have a high level in your tank, you'll welcome challenges and feel capable of meeting them. If you have a lower level in your tank, you'll feel threatened by demands on your time and energy and be more likely to experience anxiety and depression.

A low level in the tank.

As positive experiences are multiplied, your tank begins to fill. The greater the measure in the tank, the better you'll feel about yourself. You'll also find you have more energy available to meet the demands of your day-to-day life. The things which add energy to your tank come to you through an inlet line. It's attached to the tank like this:

Positives fill your tank.

Managing the Reserve Tank

The positive things which you've included in your life raise the level in your tank. Your tank will be filled by such things as knowing you handled a job well, receiving a compliment, having a good time with a friend or family member, exercise that refreshes you, or feeling capable because you really do like yourself. Other things which would fill your tank include:

- Learning something new
- Listening to music
- A walk in the park
- Accepting a compliment
- Seeing a sunset or sunrise
- Visiting with a friend
- Going to the movies
- Reading a good book
- Dancing
- Receiving a card
- Giving a gift
- Spending time alone
- Taking a long shower
- Meeting a deadline
- Exercising
- A satisfying sexual encounter
- Eating dinner out
- Eating dinner in
- Taking a class
- Restful sleep
- A hobby

These are only intended to be suggestive of the many things which can fill your tank; many more could be listed. Each person's list is very personalized, although there may be some universal fillers. To make your assessment of what's truly a filler even more complicated, some behaviors may be fillers at one point in time, but emptiers at another. For example, you might as a rule enjoy a spirited game of racquetball, but find it less than enjoyable immediately after eating a huge meal of Mexican food.

The tank also has an outlet or depletion line. Adding the depletion line to the figure makes the picture look like this:

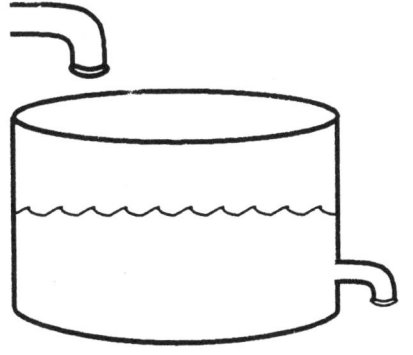

Your tank is emptied through the depletion line.

If You Can't Say No You Can't Really Say Yes

This outlet allows the tank to be emptied as you meet your day-to-day responsibilities and as you pay a price for your dissatisfactions. Involvement in the daily demands of life as well as the negative influences you endure reduce the level in your tank. Unresolved conflict or a personal attack takes something from your tank.

Other negative forces which deplete your reserve tank would include:

- A fight with your spouse or significant other
- Problems on the job
- Loss of a friend in death
- Spiritual confusion
- Breaking something you value
- Rejection of a personal project
- A disappointing sexual experience
- Receiving a cutting remark
- A stain on your new suit
- Running out of gas in your car
- Being left alone to do the yard work—again
- A bad haircut
- Meeting the usual demands of life
- Missing out on an important opportunity
- Sickness
- "Shoulds" or perfectionism
- Trauma (like a serious illness or having an automobile accident)
- Feeling isolated

Be sure to note that even your tank fillers will have an emptying effect on the measure in your tank. Moderate exercise that's within the range of your skills is one of the things which will fill your tank, but exercise uses up energy which will then be unavailable for any other use. However, such exercise will add more to the tank than is depleted, so that you'll experience a net gain in the level of your reserve tank. Time spent with your children can be very fulfilling, but the energy spent in an evening with them also depletes your tank. Hopefully, being with them is more filling than depleting, so you can experience an overall gain in the level of your tank.

In managing the reserve tank, the goal is to maximize your outcomes so as to keep your tank filled. Suppose you were to assign a value on a scale of 1 to 10 for each tank filler and depleter. Exercise might benefit you an 8 while costing you energy equivalent to 3 units. Overall you would experience a net gain of 5 units. Using alcohol to deal with stress might fill the tank 4 units, but cost 6 units because of poor sleep that night or embarrassing comments you made at a business dinner while under the influence. Overall you would experience a net loss of 2 units. In order to maintain an adequate level in your tank, you must consider the overall picture of what's filling and emptying your tank.

This movement of energy into and out of your tank creates a flow through your life. This movement of energy is essential to your feeling alive and vibrant. If there's no flow through your life, you'll feel bored and stagnant. This means that you can't just stockpile emotional energy and feel satisfied. There needs to be a constant flux in your tank if you're to be happy. The motion of energy through your reserve is absolutely necessary if you're to have a healthy sense of well-being.

Take Time to Take Inventory

If you're serious about regaining your power to choose, it will be essential for you to pay more attention to the level in your tank and to assess what's filling and emptying your tank. This means becoming aware of your energy level. Time to stop, time to reflect, is the first step toward taking action to increase what fills your tank and/or to decrease what's depleting your tank.

Many of you find it difficult to set aside a time and place to stop and check the level in your tanks. Doing so is only possible when there is relative silence, when activity is at a minimum and when you're able to take an honest look at how you feel. The hustling pace of your life may make it unlikely that you'll be able to take that kind of look at yourself without making a dedicated effort to do so.

You can't hear clearly enough to know what's going on inside your tank if you're always at work, always on the move, forever doing something for someone else, or if the television is constantly droning its noise into your life. When you slow down and listen, you can hear and respond to the strong points and the needs you see reflected in the level of your tank.

Dele was a woman who seemed to move from one troubled relationship to another. She quickly committed to the men she met, moving close to them as soon as she received anything from them that even remotely felt like love. As you would expect, she was often hurt in these relationships. The occasions when she was hurt or taken advantage of left her feeling like a victim. If you listened to her describe her view of the world, she would tell you that life happened to her. It was definitely not under her power.

If You Can't Say No You Can't Really Say Yes

She let herself be used in the relationships she entered as she gave and gave, but received little in return. Her latest love interest was typical of her experience. Her current beau would seldom reciprocate the care and concern that Dele showed him. He often made promises, but most often broke them. One Friday night he told her they would go out. "I'll pick you up at nine," he said. At midnight, when he hadn't shown up or called to tell her about any change in plans, she assumed something horrible had happened to him. She started calling hospitals. "Surely he's been hurt or he would have kept his commitment!" she thought. Later she would find out that he'd gone to a club after work with some friends and had simply forgotten to call her. Again.

Because they'd said they loved one another, Dele thought she needed to stay. When she rediscovered her *personal power to choose*, she came to see that she had several choices. Staying with this man while things remained the way they were was only one of the possible choices. She could also—

- Leave him and feel very hurt, angry and resentful.
- Leave him knowing she'd done all she could to make things work.
- Stay and firmly request change.

Like Dele, many of the people who decide to talk to friends, spouses, ministers and counselors about their exhaustion or sadness have left their tanks unattended. They have given so much to others that they are empty themselves. Often this neglect has gone on for years, perhaps even decades! They sense an emptiness which inhibits any true enjoyment of life.

When clients come for counseling and complain of these symptoms of depletion, I often have them look at what they are allowing to enter and leave their tanks. I draw the tank and explain to them the lines that fill and empty it. Then, we make a list of the things they perceive are going into and flowing out of their tanks. They also make an assessment as to the current level in their tanks.

An essential part of this process of personal assessment is being willing and able to access your feelings. Your emotional state is indicated by the feelings you're experiencing. Are you angry? Tired? Resentful? Your emotions give you important feedback as to what's going on inside. You must be able to feel them if you're to respond to the level in your reserve tank. This point is so important that an entire chapter will be dedicated to it. (See Chapter 6.)

When they see this picture for the first time, many men and women are surprised to see how little they have going into their tanks and how much they have going out of their tanks. I often hear such statements as, "No wonder I've been so tired lately!" Or, "I guess I never do things just for me." One question I regularly ask the women who come into my office is this: "What have you done for yourself in the last week that no one benefited from but you?" They often sit in stunned silence, unable to think of a thing!

Stop for a moment and assess the level of energy in your own tank. Find a quiet place. Turn off all distractions. Breathe deeply. Again. Now, answer these questions:

CHOICE EXERCISE
- Do you seem to tire easily lately?
- Is it becoming harder for you to bounce back after completing a tough job?
- Do you seem to be working harder, but accomplishing less?
- Are you seeing close friends and family members less often?
- Do you seem to have little time for yourself?
- Is your relationship with your significant someone less satisfying?
- Do you have a difficult time being still or quiet?
- Do you have to have the radio or television on when you do paperwork or dictation? (The background noise can mask the emptiness of your tank.)
- Have your sleeping patterns changed? (Sleeping a lot more or a lot less?)
- Do you have more than a year's worth of unused vacation time accumulated?

If you answered yes to two or more of these questions, your tank is probably reaching a low level which requires your immediate attention.

The Role of Boundaries

Up to this point, this description of the tank hasn't addressed the place for the exercise of personal power. The flow of energy into and out of the tank appears to be unregulated. This isn't the case. There are valves at either end of the tank which allow you to exercise choices over what goes into your tank and what flows from it. These valves are analogous to what is commonly referred to as boundaries.

Boundaries are the invisible limits between you and other people. Your boundaries dictate whom you allow to get close to you and what you allow them to do in relation to you. The strength of your boundaries is a reflection of the way in which you exercise, or fail to exercise, your power to choose.

Boundaries are equivalent to the presence of valves on the inlet and outlet lines. These valves regulate the flow of energy into and out of your life. They are located on the fill and depletion lines of the tank like this:

The valves are equivalent to boundaries

These valves reflect your willingness to exercise your *personal power to choose*. They're as functional as your ability to say, "Yes" to what you want to have flow into your tank and to say, "No" to areas where you choose not to expend your energy. Clear and effective boundaries are reflected in the precise and effective exercising of your choices! *The healthier your boundaries, the more powerful your ability to make choices will be.*

I want to say that again. If you can't effectively set boundaries, you won't experience your *personal power to choose*. Without healthy boundaries, "they" seem to control your life. Things appear to happen to you without any sense of purpose. You must set boundaries if you're to regain your power to choose!

Edna Willingham was a woman who had continually neglected her boundaries. She was the mother of a thirty-two year old son, Gavin. He was still living at home, paying no rent and contributing nothing toward the purchase of food. She washed his clothes and ironed his shirts. She and her husband had co-signed a note for a truck for Gavin and when he didn't make the payments, they "had" to make the payments for him. Her son had been to drug rehabilitation twice, paid for by his parents, and she'd recently discovered he was smoking pot again. Gavin had been in a sexual relationship with a girlfriend which resulted in the birth of a child. Edna was raising that child. She experienced little encouragement or support from her husband because he worked long hours and was seldom home except to sleep. She was tired, worn out and felt hopeless.

She felt so badly that she finally decided she needed to get some help. At our first session together, I drew her a picture of the reserve tank. As I began to explain it, she drew a deep breath, then let it out loudly. With her eyes still on the tank she said, "My tank is empty, isn't it?" She could see the problem, but even as tired as she was, Edna found it difficult to imagine changing. She saw her son's problems as evidence that she might not have done everything she could to be a good parent. She was continuing to do things for him in the hope of eventually making everything all right in his life. This was more than a full-time job. Her son was also very good at "pushing her buttons," so she did more and more for him.

Because she doubted that she'd been a proper mother to her son, Edna wouldn't set firm and consistent boundaries with Gavin. It was too important to her that she have a chance to right the wrongs she feared she might have committed in her parenting. She took more responsibility for her son's problems than did he, a sure sign of being out of balance. Still, she discontinued counseling because she wasn't yet willing to set healthier boundaries.

If these valves are left unattended, if your boundaries are neglected, three things can happen:

- You'll leave your depletion valve open too far and the tank will empty too quickly. The level in the tank will be low, perhaps chronically so.
- You'll close your inlet valve too far and your tank won't fill adequately. No matter how little goes out, if your tank is low or near empty, something *must* be coming in for the tank to fill.
- The combination of these two will leave the level of your reserve at a low level. Emotionally you'll feel depleted. Energy for the basic requirements of life will be hard to find. A chronically low level will affect you physically and spiritually as well as emotionally.

Unattended tanks don't fill. If you neglect your boundaries, the level in your tank will fall. There are always more demands made on your energy reserve than you have energy at your disposal to meet.

Since your resources are limited, you have to set limits or you'll experience a depleted tank.

The optimum for good emotional health is to keep the tank as full as possible. If your boundaries are neglected, the reserve in your tank will diminish:

Poor boundaries lead to depleted tanks.

A Story of Changed Boundaries

Mark and Frances had been married for 25 years. Mark came to see me because he was struggling with depression. He was a self-employed professional who lived with the constant fear of not being able to make enough money to support the needs of his family. His wife had gone back to work after the children were in their teens, but her help with the family finances didn't allay his worries. He continued to worry that at some point in the future there wouldn't be "enough to go around."

When he and Frances dated, Mark had been courteous and patient. They spent long hours together on dates and never had any serious arguments. However, things changed dramatically after the wedding. For the first time in his relationship with Francis, he showed her an angry and volatile aspect of his personality. If things didn't go as he thought they should, he would yell at her. Loudly. She'd never been around this kind of behavior and was quite intimidated by it. She learned to withdraw, to give in, and to avoid conflict in order to keep his angry outbursts to a minimum. As it turned out, her response of yielding only made the situation worse.

Mark's outbursts were a reflection of the emptiness of his reserve tank. When they married, he felt increased pressure to be a husband, to provide for his new bride, and to handle the problems they faced so that they could be happy. Frances never *asked* for all this protection; Mark just assumed it was his duty. The pressure he put on himself at work and at home was a constant drain on his reserve tank. By the time they came for counseling, he was empty and tired, so much so that he was showing signs of a moderate depression and had been placed on an antidepressant by his medical doctor.

Over the course of therapy, Mark learned that he could set limits at home and at work so that he could recover his power to choose. For instance, one source of drain for him professionally was accepting work that he didn't have time to complete, then feeling the strain of being unable to meet his deadlines. He learned to say no to some jobs, even though he feared he wouldn't have enough work later to be able to pay the bills. He also became more assertive at dealing with time consuming telephone calls by saying, "I'm glad you called, but I have only five minutes I can spare right now." He found that many of the run-on telephone conversations he'd endured over the years could be curtailed with no loss in goodwill and much less drain on his tank. Finally, he found that he could set more realistic time goals with his clients. Instead of always agreeing to their schedule, he could often negotiate with them for a completion time with which they were content, but which put him under much less pressure.

Things at home were slower to change. Mark's view of his role of husband required him to make everything go smoothly. That's a tremendously difficult task to accomplish! The weight of it was enough to make him tired. His expectations of perfection caused him to be critical of most everything that went on at home. His attitude seemed to say, "I know that you want a perfect family as much as I do, so I'll point out your faults. Then you can take the steps necessary to rectify your imperfections and help us reach our goal." His approach was unrealistic and stressful for himself and his entire family.

Mark came by this model for manhood honestly. This was the way his father had lived. He'd been an apt student of his father's attitude and learned to treat people with judgment and criticism because that's what he'd lived with when he was growing up at home. Even though Mark knew how much he'd hated the way he never seemed to measure up to his father's expectations, being demanding was the only way he knew to live.

In the process of living out this philosophy, Mark alienated his wife and children. They saw him not as a benevolent nurturer of family life, but as a hard-fisted tyrant who was never pleased. The perfect family he desired escaped him. Still, he found it difficult to change. When you've followed the same job description for over a quarter of a century, it's hard to put yourself out of a job!

A turning point in Mark's relationship with his family came when two unrelated events occurred the fall after he and his wife had first sought counseling. First, his oldest daughter went off to college and almost immediately sought counseling because of her long-held anger at her father. Mark found it devastating that his relationship with his daughter had been so negative that she felt compelled to seek therapy.

The second event occurred one night when he and Frances were about to go to bed. Mark blew up at her because the sheets she'd put on the bed smelled soured. When he discovered the smell, he began to yell and was verbally abusive. Frances had had enough. She'd been a participant in a women's support group and was learning to set healthy limits. She firmly told him that she hadn't intentionally put smelly sheets on the bed. She admitted that she wasn't perfect and emphasized that she was weary of attempting to appear faultless. She encouraged him to change the sheets himself if he wasn't pleased with them, but that she would no longer tolerate his abusive outbursts. Then she left the room.

Mark was stunned. All of this was new behavior for Francis. She'd said over the years that she didn't like his tirades, but she'd never said it quite like this. He didn't know what to say, so he said nothing. He changed the sheets himself. Later, they went to bed. They weren't on the best of terms at this point, but he wasn't yelling.

They began to talk more about the pressures he felt. Both Mark and Frances gave each other more freedom to make choices. Slowly Mark began to let go of the expectation of orchestrating a perfect family. This was a long and difficult process. It involved going back into his family history and doing much healing work on himself. The roots of his perfectionism stretched back to the expectations his mother and father had of him as a boy. Part of improving his relationship with his wife and children was to heal the wounds he felt from his parents. (More will be said in later chapters about this process of healing past hurts.)

Mark's marriage to Frances was enhanced as the level in his tank rose. Setting the limits at work and letting go of the inhuman and unattainable expectation of providing a faultless home life allowed him to take care of himself, leading to a rise in the amount of energy he had in reserve.

Changes Bring Benefits

Many of you women who are studying this material have been taught to think of everyone else first. The model shown to you by your mother and the other important women in your life dictated that the needs of your husband, children and friends come before your own needs. Many of you men reading this grew up watching your fathers leave—off to work or to fish or to drink. Your model of manhood dictates that you be absent! You're not there for the people in your life. But worse, being absent means you won't be present for yourself either. If you're to feel the potency of your power to choose, you must make renewed efforts to be in your own life. You have the chance now to choose the roles you're willing to play instead of continuing to read a script that was given to you in childhood.

Stop. Ask yourself how you feel. Wait until you know the answer, or at least until you have a clue. Note the level of energy in your reserve tank. Then you can say, "Yes" and, "No" as you need to.

Changing the rules governing the filling and emptying of your tank can be difficult, yet rewarding work. Some of the people around you may object to the changes because they've benefited so much from the energy which in the past flowed freely from your tank. They may resist your efforts at change. You'll have to be sure enough of your desire to change and sick enough of the emptiness you feel to stick by your guns.

In many cases, even slight adjustments at each valve can allow you to increase the level in your reserve tank to a more satisfying level. Adding thirty minutes a day to do something just for yourself can pay big dividends. Saying no to working late at the office every night, resigning from one of the committees you serve on, or saying no to your wife when she suggests an evening shopping for plants when you aren't in the mood can be ways to set limits on what goes out of the tank.

As the level in the tank rises, energy and a positive sense of well-being also increase. A sense of truly being alive returns.

It doesn't come easily. Often the road to a fuller, more vibrant life is difficult and long. But change can happen.

If You Can't Say No You Can't Really Say Yes

POWER TO CHOOSE: Find a place away from the pressure of work and the noise of people and the television. Close your eyes for a moment and breathe deeply. Once more. Now, use these questions to assess the condition of your tank:

What is the current level in your reserve tank?

_____

_____

What has happenened today that significantly filled your tank?

_____

_____

What has happened today that significantly depleted your tank?

_____

_____

What one change would make the biggest difference in what fills and empties your tank?

_____

_____

What steps can you take now to begin reclaiming your boundaries and allow for an increase in the level of your tank?

_____

_____

Can you speak with conviction the following affirmation?
I am ready to exercise my personal power to choose by taking charge of my boundaries!

3

JUST SAY, "NO!"
Exploring the vital role of boundaries

MOLLY AND MIKE had been married for seven years. One Monday night in November, Molly asked Mike to go with her to a "moonlight madness" sale at the mall. She felt a need for his companionship since he'd been away much of the last three weeks on business trips. She wanted to draw closer to her husband and suggested this shared trip.

Mike had planned to stay home tonight and watch the football game on television. He had his drinks and his snacks all laid out on the table in the den. He was really looking forward to seeing these two, division-leading teams play each other. When Molly asked him to go with her, his first response to himself was, "No way!" But he knew that he'd been gone a lot lately. And what she was asking for seemed so simple. So he reluctantly said yes.

The entire time he was at the mall, Mike was feeling upset and withdrawn. He hadn't admitted his emotions, but they were there just the same. He thought Molly had taken advantage of him. Molly continued to ask if something was wrong, but each time she asked, he said, "No." He was trying to be a good husband. Besides, he reasoned, Molly would just be angry or clam up if he told her how he felt.

Molly became more and more frustrated. At about half-time in the game, Mike mentioned that he was ready to go home. Molly exploded. "You haven't wanted to be here from the first minute we arrived," she said. "You've been impossible to deal with all evening, and now you want to go home!"

Mike said, "I *knew* you would be like this. You're so unreasonable!" They marched to the car in a storm and drove home in silence. When they got to the house, they didn't speak and slept in separate rooms. Mike watched the rest of the game, but didn't enjoy it very much. The next morning, they both felt tired and angry. A hostile silence pushed them apart.

What Are Boundaries?

What went wrong between Molly and Mike? Why did things go so badly between them when they both had such good intentions? The issue is simple to pinpoint, but difficult to change. Mike and Molly didn't establish healthy boundaries.

As you read in the last chapter, boundaries are the invisible limits you set in your life. Your limits determine whom you let get close, how close you let others get, and what you choose to do in your relationship with them. Boundaries let you know who *you* are and who *they* are. Without clear boundaries, you'll get this confused. Either others will control you or you'll attempt to gain control of others. Your boundaries keep you intact by helping you focus on yourself and let go of the behavior of others.

Remember that boundaries are like valves on your tank which determine what goes in and what goes out of your tank. Balanced boundaries are essential to your being able to exercise healthy choices:

Healthy boundaries result in filled tanks.

You weren't born with boundaries. You learned about your limits in interaction with others in your world. Initially your parents are the most powerful influence in the formulation of your boundaries. At first all of us were merged with our parents, unable to determine where we ended and they began. When as an infant you cried, they came to assist. When you were hungry, they supplied food. When you were wet, they made you dry. When you were in distress, they provided comfort.

Just Say, "No"

Slowly you discovered that *you* were not *them*. You discovered your own feet and hands. You learned to touch, carry, and move things. You exercised your ability to be autonomous. You discovered your own ability to say, "No!" In short, you found that you had boundaries.

In healthy families, an atmosphere is provided for the development of clear boundaries. Children in such families are allowed to feel, think, and act for themselves. Parents who are functional allow their children to explore the world for themselves, without shoulds, oughts and judgment. This freedom is essential to learning healthy boundaries.

Children need to be able to talk about their reality and have it confirmed as reality, at least for them. A parent doesn't have to agree with a child to be able to affirm the child's view of the world. For instance, if a child shows up at his parent's bedside at two in the morning because he's afraid of ghosts, a parent can say, "You're really scared, aren't you!" without believing in ghosts. It's not very helpful for a child to hear, "Go back to bed! Don't be afraid! There's no such things as ghosts!"

If as a child you weren't allowed to have and express your own reality, you'll likely find it difficult to accept your feelings and perceptions now. You probably find it difficult to trust your "gut," that part of you that senses intuitively what is going on in your world.

One of the core elements of developing your power to choose is the ability to make your own choices, even if they're "wrong." Without making incorrect choices, there's no learning about appropriate choices. Children who blow their allowance on a toy that they didn't really want can learn impulse control. They learn that saving for something better or different is more to their benefit. Mistakes are part of the learning process.

The central message of this freedom to choose is self-knowledge and self-acceptance. Without this liberty to know and express yourself, it's impossible to cultivate healthy boundaries. If you haven't learned to read what goes on inside of yourself, you won't know when it's time to set a limit.

Many of you grew up in families where you weren't given this freedom to explore the limits of your world. You didn't have the freedom to feel afraid or hurt without the judgments of a parent. You may have been told, "Boys don't cry!" or, "You're not hurt!" You wondered if you had any sense at all, because it sure *felt* like hurt even if mom and/or dad said it wasn't.

If You Can't Say No You Can't Really Say Yes

The Importance of Balanced Boundaries

You can take back your personal power by establishing and standing behind clear, healthy boundaries. You have the freedom to say, "No!" When you're willing to feel the needs inside of you, you can begin the process of meeting those needs.

Your boundaries will either help or hinder you, depending upon how rigid or loose they are and how productively they serve you. Your boundaries can let others get too close so that you feel you're losing yourself or they can keep others at a distance so that you make little meaningful contact with anyone in your world. The key is to find a healthy balance between these two extremes.

As a way of illustrating three different kinds of boundaries, think of three very different houses on the same mythical block. The first house is a structure with no windows and doors. When the house was built, holes were left in the walls for windows and doors, but they were never installed. These permanent holes in the wall allow bugs, animals, and other humans to come into and out of your house as they chose. There would be no sense of safety or privacy. What you do and anything you own could be seen by anyone who cared to look. You couldn't be alone since there's no place in such a house to have that kind of protected solitude. You couldn't feel safe when you were at home because someone could easily come inside and hurt you or steal your things. That's what it's like to have boundaries which are too loose.

Limits like these which let others get too close are called *diffuse*. They are too loose. In a family with diffuse boundaries there's a sense of stickiness. The Bendix family had this kind of boundaries. Mother and dad did everything with the children. No one in the family was allowed to close the door to his or her room. During one of their counseling sessions, the eight year old son, who always had to sit in mom's lap, picked up his mom's hand in his and picked *his* teeth with *her* fingernail. That's enmeshed!

If you have diffuse boundaries, you'll feel vulnerable and fearful. You'll be anxious that you're losing yourself. There will be a sense that others are repeatedly taking advantage of you. One man who had boundaries which were too open described himself as a Ping-Pong ball and his wife as a vacuum cleaner. Whenever he was near her, he feared she would consume him. His fears caused him to distance from her to avoid being "swallowed up whole."

At the other extreme, imagine a house at the opposite end of the block that's built like a fortress and has walls of concrete which are three feet thick. There are no windows so no light or fresh air can get inside. The only way in and out of the place is through a door about the size of a doggy door. Anyone who wants to go out or come inside has to get down on his hands and knees and crawl. In this house you wouldn't be bothered with drop-in visitors. In fact, the problem is just the opposite: no one comes to visit because it's just too hard to get inside.

This type of boundaries is called *rigid*. When your boundaries are rigid, you'll feel cut off and alone. You'll seek to keep everyone at a distance. There's little opportunity for closeness. Important needs for connection and intimacy go unmet. Contact with others is limited and dissatisfying.

The Hobbs family had very rigid boundaries. Things had to be done in a specific and never-questioned way. There was very little tolerance for variation. There were no displays of affection; that would have required contact. "I love you" was a phrase never spoken between them. One of the family secrets, revealed by the couple's only child, a teenager, in a private counseling session, was that mom and dad didn't sleep in the same room. Their family had a look of togetherness to outside observers, but their boundaries were so tight that they seldom made any sort of meaningful contact. They really didn't even know each other.

In the middle of the block, between these two extremes, there's another kind of house which symbolizes healthy boundaries. This house has large doors which open and close and big windows that let in fresh air and sunlight. The doors and windows can be opened or closed by the people living inside the house. At night they can be locked. If someone knocks at the door, the people inside the house can decide whether or not to admit her. When they go to bed, the family inside the house feels safe because the windows and doors can be locked to keep out unwanted visitors or intruders. It's easy for people outside the family to connect with the family inside the house because the doors open wide, inviting others inside.

The type of boundaries suggested by this house are called *clear*. When your boundaries are clear, you can say, "Yes" and, "No" as it reflects your needs. If you want to reclaim your power to choose, you'll have to become more aware of your needs and set appropriate limits in order to maximize the level in your reserve tank.

Clarifying Boundaries

Since your boundaries are invisible, you can't actually see them. However, evidence of the condition of your boundaries can be seen in your interaction with people and in what you choose or refuse to do in response to others. If you find yourself consistently saying yes to things you would like to have declined, your boundaries are probably too loose. On the other hand, if you most often say no to requests for your time or for interaction with others, you've probably cut yourself off from others, evidence of boundaries which are too tight. Either of these extremes will result in a low level in your tank. Boundaries that are too loose will lead to your saying yes too often, losing too much of yourself. Boundaries that are too tight will result in your saying no too often, robbing yourself of interactions with others that can fill your tank.

For best results, you'll need to recognize that your boundaries:
- Entail learning to take care of yourself.
- Will change when you experience again your *personal power to choose*.
- Grow stronger as you learn to take inventory of your reserve tank.
- Will change as you learn to honor what you want and need.

If you learn to set boundaries firmly and without apology, you can change your life. Please take the time to read that last sentence again and contemplate its meaning more fully. When you give yourself permission to acknowledge your needs, then set healthy limits, changes *will* occur. Tanks which have been emptied can be filled again.

Sam and his children are caught in a dissatisfying and tank-emptying cycle. Sam is a non-custodial, single father who sees his children one night a week and every other weekend. Because he doesn't see his children often, and because he wants to be a good father, he puts tremendous pressure on himself to make his children's visits go well. The visits usually begin with his letting his children get away with too much. They yell or argue or demand from him. They talk him into going out to eat even though he has food at home and doesn't have extra money to take them out. As the visit progresses, he often begins to feel angry and empty. He yells at his children, yet would tell you that he doesn't want to parent that way. In order to guard what he has left in his tank, he says, "No" too often in an attempt to regain control of his children. This sets up a battle that leaves him exhausted and depressed at the end of every visit.

While he can still remain flexible and allow for change, there's no reason for Sam to allow his tank to be emptied on each visit. His depleted tank results in a bad experience for him and his children. His visits with his children would go much better if he would set healthy limits with them from the time they arrive and enforce those limits in a loving, firm manner through out their visit. Saying no to his children about eating out may seem like a simple thing, too simple to make any difference in his life. The truth is, saying no is the way we learn to honor ourselves and is the first step toward changing our relationships with others.

Your tank fills to a higher level when you say no.

Learning to take inventory, listening to our needs, and speaking up to set healthy boundaries can improve relationships between men and women in committed relationships. A new willingness to set limits can drastically change the look of a marriage. Eleanor was sure that her marriage was over. When she came to counseling, she saw no hope at all for improving her relationship with her husband. All she wanted was out. She couldn't have imagined that only a few months later she would be happier in her marriage than she'd ever been.

When she first came for treatment, her therapist did nothing but listen to her. Eleanor was so disgusted with her marriage that she had nothing good to say about her husband. Step one for her was to allow her to admit without judgment how badly she felt about her relationship. Before she could make a wise decision about the direction her life could take, she needed to admit to herself just how badly she felt. Her initial assignment was to write every day for twenty to thirty minutes about how angry, hurt and disappointed she felt. The counselor told her to let her negative feelings "run all over you like liquid. Feel the sensations. It's time to stop pretending!"

When she returned the next week, Eleanor reported that she'd been unable to carry out her assignment. She said she "couldn't write those horrible things down" that she'd been thinking. First, she didn't want to admit that she actually felt so badly. Second, she felt guilty feeling so negatively about her husband. "After all," she rationalized, "he doesn't beat me. He doesn't drink. He's good to the children. He's really not so awful." The counselor emphasized again how important it was for her to take this step. Only when she faced the truth of how she felt could she begin to experience change. After that second meeting, she left the session convinced of the need to be honest.

And she was! The next week she returned with a notebook full of venom! She wouldn't even open her journal because it seemed to her the contents were too toxic. She stuck with the writing and after three weeks, she began to feel more accepting of her feelings. She also began to see a pattern.

The things she was most upset about often had to do with things her husband had failed to do. He didn't help with dinner. He watched television instead of entertaining the children. He didn't hug her just for the sake of a hug. He would go to work, then come home and camp out on the couch.

"What would happen if you asked him for some help?" the therapist wondered out loud at their next session.

"He probably wouldn't help me. If he hasn't been able to see that I've needed help, why would he start helping me just because I asked?" It's quite common for us to have this, "Can't he/she see what I need?" mentality about our mates. Sometimes it may appear that our partners go out of their way *not* to pay attention. It may seem that he or she is "blind in one eye and can't see out of the other," as my grandmother was fond of saying.

The truth is that sometimes our spouses aren't paying attention. Or they haven't thought about what you might want. They may fail to listen. They may not have heard, or if they heard, they forgot. They may never have been told and have been unable to read the clues you expected them to decipher. The bottom line is that you'll have to tell the other person specifically what you want if you want him/her to respond.

While Eleanor still wasn't convinced that telling her husband her needs would make any difference, she saw that she had nothing to lose. She took the risk to ask for her husband's assistance. It was a risk because she could have been blown off, rejected, ignored or yelled at when she asked for his help.

Eleanor found that when her husband knew what she wanted him to do to help her, he was willing to be involved. He would work with her to prepare dinner. He ran the vacuum. He would get the children into the tub and on to bed. You might argue that he "should" have been able to see what needed to be done and do it, and you might have a point. The positive thing was that once he knew what she wanted, he was willing to be involved.

As her husband responded favorably to her requests, a strange thing began to happen. Eleanor found her feelings of love for him returning. As her tank filled, she became more comfortable with touching and shared closeness. It wasn't long before she was initiating a sexual encounter, something she hadn't done in years.

After only a handful of sessions, Eleanor ended therapy. A year later her counselor made a follow-up call to see if Eleanor and her husband had maintained their changes and she found that they'd in fact done so. The counselor never met with Eleanor's husband, but he did call her once several months after the last session with his wife to thank her "for all you've done for my wife."

What happened? What made it possible for Eleanor's emotions to change so drastically? One important answer to that question is that she listened to what she needed and set some firm, healthy boundaries to get it. She learned to say, "Would you help me with this?" She saw that it was okay for her to say, "No, I don't believe I want to do that right now." When she was able to regain her power to choose, she didn't feel used or taken advantage of any more. Feeling used will empty a reserve tank faster than just about anything else. "Used" is how you'll feel when you haven't set good boundaries.

Learning Your NBCs

Your boundaries aren't an isolated aspect of your life. In order to set appropriate limits with others, you must recognize that boundaries travel in a triad. Setting boundaries is preceded by an awareness of a need that you have. Once you've recognize the need, you can then set a clear boundary to help you meet that need. Finally, consequences put power into your boundaries. Your boundaries are only as strong and useful as the consequences you bring to bear to back them up. The process can be pictured like this:

If You Can't Say No You Can't Really Say Yes

Need ➡ Boundary ➡ Consequence

The process of establishing healthy limits begins when you stop to assess what it is you need. This implies that you've stopped or at least paused long enough to take an inventory and have some idea about what your needs are. You'll have to ask yourself how you feel and what you desire, then listen very carefully for the answer. Conscious effort at first is the only way to hear your needs. It takes silence and stillness to be able to read the level in your reserve tank. As time goes on, the connection between your awareness and your tank grow stronger, so that you're aware of the condition of your tank sooner with less strenuous effort.

Examples of some needs you might have would be:
- A need for some time alone
- A need for exercise
- A need for rest
- A need for a special, intense time to focus on your work
- A need for companionship
- A need for sexual closeness
- A need to be still and quiet

After you become aware of your need, you'll have to set the limits that will enable you to meet that particular need. When you're in a relationship, the process of negotiation to get your needs met begins at this point. If you need time for exercise, but you've already agreed to have dinner with your partner's parents, problem-solving begins as to how you'll find the time and space to meet that need. You might exercise before or after the dinner. You might go for a 40 minute walk instead of playing tennis for two hours, but schedule time for tennis the next day. You could cancel out on dinner, but of course that choice has the potential for an outcome that you might not enjoy. (The fact that canceling your dinner plans might have negative consequences doesn't mean you can't choose to do so, only that there's a price to pay if you do. It may be, however, that for today, exercise is important enough that you'll want to change the plans.)

What you do as you set boundaries is ask for what you want, then deal with what you get. In the words of those immortal philosophers from England, "You can't always get what you want!" But you won't get much at all until you set some limits and begin the process of discussing options.

Just Say, "No"

Just because you tell another person you want something doesn't mean that he or she has to comply. You may ask your boss for a raise and be turned down. You could ask your wife for a passionate, sexual experience and be put off. You might request your husband's help in painting the living room and be denied. Speaking up is essential, but it doesn't guarantee that you'll get a yes. Other people have choices, too. You don't have power to make *their* choices.

If you get a no, it's at that point that the process of negotiation begins in earnest. Can you stay with this job without a raise? Would a couple of significant perks make you feel more satisfied? Would a change in responsibility or a company car be an alternative to a raise? If your wife says no to a sexual encounter tonight, could you agree on a rendezvous the next morning? If not now, when might your husband be willing to assist you in painting? What would have to happen to create an outcome where you both get what you want?

The third part of your NBCs is consequences. Consequences are the part of this triad that put "teeth" in your boundaries. What are you willing to do or say in response to an unmet boundary? How strongly do you believe in what you've asked for? Are you willing to back up your words with something that gives them strength?

You have a need to be a responsible and effective parent. You also want to watch your selected program in peace. Your four-year-old son is playing with the volume control on the television set, interrupting the program you and some guests are watching. Your boundary to your son is, "Don't touch that knob again!" But you don't back it up. Instead, you say, "Don't touch that again! Did you hear me? Are you listening to me? I don't know why you won't mind me! You do that once more and you'll be in big trouble. I'm going to count to three. One, two.... Do you want me to say,'Three?'" Twenty minutes later you're angry and your guests have given up on watching the show.

What happened? You stated what you wanted, but didn't back it up with consequences. You could have given your words some force by using a series of consequences. "Jeremy, if you touch that television again, you'll spend two minutes in time out." And if he does, you follow through. When you respond in this way, your boundaries are being enforced. If that consequence isn't strong enough to enforce the boundary, you could move on to sending Jeremy to his room, or putting him to bed early.

The consequences you employ must be strong enough to back up your boundary. Without powerful consequences, your boundary requests are nothing but attempts to beg another person to do what you want. You may even see yourself in a whiny voice, down on your knees, saying, "Ple-e-e-ease don't do that!?" You feel no personal power. You have little sense that your life is your own.

When you're willing to take charge of your choices, your tank can fill. And you have the satisfaction of knowing that you took care of yourself. Few things in life feel better than that!

You must remember that your boundaries are for you. They aren't designed to control the behavior of other people. Your limits are your own. They must reflect your power to choose, or they'll be of little value. Consider the case of a woman who had broken up with a man she dated for two years. She came to see that the relationship was one that emptied rather than filled her tank, so she broke it off and asked him not to call her. However, he continued to call, sometimes two or three times a day. The woman says to a friend, "I asked him not to call, but he won't honor my boundary." Can you see how she's continuing to give her power away? If it's her boundary, *she's* the one who has to honor it, not the man she broke up with. When the phone rings and she finds it's the man she no longer wishes to talk to, she can remind him of her request. If he continues to talk, she can hang up. Remember: You're the one who is in charge of your limits.

Consequences typically start small and grow stronger and/or larger with further violations. Sometimes a boundary can be enforced with minimal consequences. There's no reason to swat a fly with a sledgehammer! However, if you're breaking up a concrete driveway, you need a sledgehammer. Use the correct tool for the job. If you're a man or woman involved with a person who is clearly abusing alcohol, you might set a boundary that you want to live in a sober, alcohol-free atmosphere. The first consequence might be a reminder. The second might be making an appointment to talk to a counselor, whether he or she goes with you or not. The third might be attending Al-Anon meetings. Down the line you may have to end the relationship if the alcohol abuse continues.

Reasons You Don't Say No

You define yourself when you say no. Saying no allows you to realize and exercise your *personal power to choose*. Setting limits permits you to feel good about yourself. Establishing boundaries reduces the amount of tension you feel because you take responsibility for your part of any issue and encourage others to do the same.

Just Say, "No"

Your tank empties when you fail to say no.

Saying no allows you to let go of control, while setting healthy limits for yourself.

If setting limits can make you feel so energized and leads to such positive outcomes in your life, why don't you set boundaries more effectively? Why is it that you fail to say no? There are several reasons.

First, you may not have said no because you didn't know you could. Living in an enmeshed, alcoholic, or chaotic home may have taught you that you couldn't say what you wanted and receive a healthy response. Saying no or simply asking for clarification may have prompted a shameful put down or a physical attack from an emotionally hurting and wounded parent. In such settings it's easier, perhaps even life-saving, not to speak up.

Helen grew up with a violent, alcoholic father. Many of her childhood memories involve some senseless act of violence. She remembers running to check the refrigerator when she heard dad arrive because she wanted to be sure dad had enough soda to mix his drinks. She recalls washing dishes and for no reason being hit from the blind side by her inebriated father. She learned to keep her thoughts and feelings to herself. Her boundaries, as well as those of all of her siblings, were repeatedly violated by her father. Years later she carried these old prohibitions against setting limits into new relationships. These old rules strained her marriage because they implied a lack of trust for her spouse. Helen needed to unlearn her old family rules before she could regain her power to chose.

Second, you may have hesitated to say no because you're left feeling guilty when you do so. The person to whom you said no may even help feed the guilty feelings in you. "What do you mean, you can't help?" Perhaps the response is just a sigh or one of *those* looks.

If You Can't Say No You Can't Really Say Yes

Changing often means learning to deal with the dissatisfaction of others which is aimed at you when you say no.

One of the most depressed women I ever worked with was a minister's wife who believed she had to continue to give even though the reserve in her tank had long since been exhausted. Her husband worked a full-time job, then preached on Sundays for a small church. This demanding schedule meant that he was seldom home, and when he was, he offered her little help and support.

At his urging they'd taken in three foster children in addition to the three they'd conceived together. Saying "they" had taken them in is really a fabrication. Over the years she'd assumed almost total responsibility for the children. Her husband worked until late each evening, returning home after everyone was in bed. She did the physical work necessary to care for the little ones, ran the carpool, solved the problems, helped with homework, dished out the discipline and got them through baths and into the bed.

When she came for counseling she wasn't sleeping, was "tired all the time," was short-tempered with the children, and cried at the least provocation. She felt so empty she scarcely could get going every day, but she hadn't been able to say no to taking on further responsibility.

The main reason she kept taking in more children was her desire not to disappoint her husband. She was no fool; she could see how tired she was. She was also aware that she wasn't doing her best parenting. However, she couldn't bear the thought of her husband's saying, "What do you mean, you can't care for one more child?" She discontinued counseling because she couldn't allow herself to face the disappointment of letting her husband down. She gave in in advance to a guilt trip she thought he would aim at her.

You'll have to remember that there are two sides to guilt: First, someone lays down a guilt trip and *then* you pick it up. Just because he lays it down doesn't mean you have to pick it up. You can choose to let it lie. When you do so, you take steps toward regaining your power of choice.

A third reason you may have hesitated to say no is that you've lived with a philosophy that there's a lack of power available in the world. You may have believed that there wasn't enough power to go around. Because power is so often thought of as being a scarce commodity, you may have focused on taking power from others or on making sure no one takes power from you! Men try to take power from women. Women seek to get power from men. Bosses seek to control

Just Say, "No"

their employees. Employees want to have the power their bosses possess. What a mess this becomes!

You need to accept a new reality: a gospel of bountiful provision. There's no lack of power. You live in a world of unlimited resources! There's as much power available to you as you need. No one has to fight anyone else for power; there's plenty to go around. There's no reason to worry that you've taken someone else's power, so you don't have to feel hesitant to speak your mind.

A fourth reason you may not say no is that you may see the issue as being petty. You may even say to yourself, "I shouldn't even be upset about this. It's such a small thing." If your spouse has his or her own tube of toothpaste, but constantly takes and doesn't return yours, you may be irritated. You might say to yourself, "It's no big deal. I'll just look for mine. It's not worth being upset about." If it truly is "no big deal," then you'll get over it quickly or find that you aren't bothered by it at all. However, if you store negative feelings as a result, it probably is a big enough deal to talk about and an indication that the issues do need to be discussed. Regaining your choices comes when you take the risk to discuss it.

A fifth reason you might not set limits is that you think that the other person should know what you want. You may reason that if you have to ask for something, you wouldn't really enjoy receiving it. You may feel like a beggar. "If she loved me, she would know what I want." "If he loved me, I wouldn't even have to ask." Even if the other person responds favorably to your request and gives you what you've requested, you may still reject the attempt because it was only given in response to your asking for it.

It *does* feel good when someone gives you something for which you didn't have to ask. Such serendipitous gifts make our lives richer. However, asking before receiving need not make the gift unenjoyable. A requested back rub can still be relaxing and make you feel appreciated.

Finally, you may have difficulty saying no due to your religious values. You may have been taught that being a spiritual person means that you do for others even when you (1) don't feel like it, (2) have nothing in your tank to give, or (3) aren't sure it would be the best thing for the other person if you *did* give to him. These are all perversions of the concept of servanthood.

Brenda was a concerned Christian mother who wrestled with how to be a good parent to her son, Luke, who was on drugs—again. She and her husband had suffered through the problems related to their son's addiction for the last four years. They'd nagged him, loved him, argued with him, and made arrangements for him to go to treatment. Luke eventually made it through high school, even though it took him an extra year. Brenda thought Luke was finally clean, but she found new evidence that he was using drugs once again, and had been doing so for some time.

In the past, Brenda's first response had been to jump in and begin giving again. Help him. Get him to treatment. Snatch him from the terrible problems she'd seen drugs could cause. This time Brenda was slower to respond. Maybe helping her son was the wrong thing to do. The counselors they'd met with during Luke's treatment had used the word "enabling" to describe action which concerned parents often take which actually allows the addiction to continue. Besides, after fighting with these problems for so long, Brenda had nothing more in her tank to give. So she made a different choice. At first she didn't feel good about it because it felt so uncaring not to respond actively to her son. But as time went on, she saw the wisdom in a new course of action.

She expressed her concern to her son lovingly and freely. However, she didn't offer help financially. When her son was arrested for possession, she didn't bail him out. Eventually her son went to trial represented by a court appointed lawyer. He was convicted and placed on probation. It hurt Brenda to see her son go through this, but she remained convinced that things would change only when Luke took responsibility for his life. If Brenda stepped in to rescue Luke from the consequences of his actions, she would *hurt* rather than *help* her son. With this new insight, she was able to stick to her choice to say no to her son. More will be said in Chapter 18 about balancing your spiritual values as you regain your power to choose.

Reasons You Don't Say Yes

If you're to be healthy and have a high level of energy in your reserve tank, you must be able and willing to say yes to those things which can fill your tank. Even if you learn to limit what goes out, you must also fill the reserve tank if the level is to increase. You'll have to say yes as well as no. However, often you don't say yes frequently enough to fill the tank. There are several reasons why this might be the case.

First, you may not think you have time. "I didn't have time." I've heard lots of people say that. Like they had less of what the rest of us have more of. The truth is, you have the same amount of time as

Just Say, "No"

The level in your tank rises as you say yes to fillers.

everyone else. The difference from person to person in what you're able to accomplish is in how you choose to use your time. In fact, it might make more sense to say that you can't afford *not* to provide the things which fill your tank, so you take the steps necessary to make time.

Second, you may be following old rules that restrict the things to which you can say yes. If you follow a rule which says, "Don't let other people get too close," then you'll avoid the fulfilling nature of quality relationships with others. Some dads spend so much time at work or gone to play that they don't build healthy relationships with their families. Some women who have been hurt by men construct a protective wall around themselves, keeping their partner away. Giving yourself permission to be close to others will allow you to receive the benefits that close relationships can bring.

Updating the rules you live by may be difficult work. Some rules change rather easily, while others may seem to run to your very core. Giving this second kind up can seem extremely threatening. For instance, how close you let someone get, emotionally or physically, will often bring up painful or troublesome issues for you. It may take concentration and focus to change some of your rules.

Third, you might have failed to say yes because you didn't perceive you had a choice. You may have felt like you were "stuck between a rock and a hard place." You may not have known that you had a vote when it comes to choosing the direction your life will take. If you feel forced, you may say no to something you would really like to have done if you'd felt you had a choice. It's important to recognize that you do have choices.

You may have to do some very pointed and painful work in order to once again recognize your choices. You may have to construct a list of options before you respond to a situation. Asking yourself, "What other options do I have?" may help you identify additional possibilities. Brainstorming by making a list of alternative responses, without judgment, may be a helpful response to your feeling stuck.

Saying yes can fill your tank. When you open the filler valve and allow energy to flow into your tank, the level in your tank can rise. It's important to say no to things that deplete you, but it's just as important to say yes to some things that can fill you up.

Suggestions for Setting Boundaries

If you are to increase or regain your *personal power to choose*, you must learn to set clearer, firmer boundaries. You'll need to set them sooner, before you're empty or extremely angry. You'll be most effective when you can learn to communicate them calmly and clearly. Here are some suggestions to help you as you practice.

1. Stay in touch with yourself emotionally. This step in the process is vital! The way you handle the limits on your tank can't change until you become more aware of how you feel. If you don't listen to your emotions, you'll miss some important cues. Take time to stop and determine how you feel. If you find yourself feeling frustrated, tired, used or angry, a boundary has probably been violated. Your neighbor borrowed your hammer two months ago and hasn't returned it. You need it for a repair job you're doing one Saturday, but when you go to retrieve it, no one is at home. You find yourself borrowing a hammer from another of your neighbors because you can't use your own. Take a moment to really ask yourself, "How do I feel?" Listen and respond appropriately.

2. If you aren't enjoying something that you usually enjoy, you've probably allowed a boundary to be violated. If you normally like to play tennis, but find this game or this partner to be unenjoyable, a faulty boundary may be to blame. Did you feel coerced into playing? Does this particular playing partner leave you feeling uncomfortable with his play or his reaction to missed shots?

3. Sometimes your tank will be low because you've said no too often. You may have avoided tank fillers like exercise, intimate communication with another person, or doing something for others. It's not enough to know that your tank is too low; you'll need to go a step further and ascertain *why* it's low. Then you'll need to take action. The level in your tank can increase when you take steps to alter the choices which have been limiting the flow of energy into your tank.

4. When you identify a place where a boundary needs to be set, do it clearly, using as few words as possible. If you choose to give an explanation, you may do so. However, reasons don't have to be given. Remember that, "No." is a complete sentence!

You don't have to justify every boundary you erect. Waiting until you've got it all figured out before you set a boundary can set you up to be hurt. It's enough to say, "No." for the moment and if you want, you can add, "I'm not even sure why, but I choose not to for now!"

5. When you set a boundary, do so without anger if possible. You'll communicate what you want more effectively if you'll do so before you're extremely angry. However, if being angry is the only way you can set a boundary, do it in anger for now. Learning to set limits without inappropriate anger is part of the growth process.

6. Don't expect others always to like the changes in your boundaries. Changing boundaries is like adjusting the thermostat in your home. If you become cold or hot and change the setting, someone else may object. Others may even attempt to push the thermostat back to its previous setting. A contest of wills can follow. Altering your boundaries won't always cause conflict, but it can.

7. Your new boundaries will be tested. Be prepared to reassert your intention to keep the new limits in place. Don't expect all the other people in your world to accept your new limits without question.

8. Some people in your life will actually applaud your desire to communicate and stand up for what you want. Your spouse, friends, or co-workers may welcome the fact that they no longer have to guess about what you want from them. Don't be surprised if the quality of your relationships actually improves when you learn to speak up for yourself.

Standing Firm With Your Boundaries

There's always inertia which must be overcome when relationship changes are attempted. The tendency to want things to remain the same is strong. Often, no matter how hard you try, relationships with others may suffer initially as you set new boundaries for yourself. Like a surgeon who operates on a patient to remove a tumor, you must be willing to risk hurting another person in order to change the relationship patterns. Wounding isn't the *intention* of boundary changes, but it's an outcome you must be willing to risk.

One young man I know tried diligently to change things between himself and his parents. Bill began with small, hesitant steps to separate himself from his parents. At 25 years of age he still spent much of his time attempting to please his mom and dad. They were such a big part of his life that he felt uncomfortable with their closeness, often feeling smothered and controlled. Yet he found it difficult to detach from them. They lived in another city, but would call almost daily. They dropped in without notice. They had a key to his house which they used as they wished. With regularity, they passed harsh judgments on his life, his employment, his religious views, and his dating relationships. For the sake of "getting along," he'd allowed their relationship to continue in this way for years.

Things came to a head between Bill and his parents when he became serious about a woman of whom they didn't approve. Sue was a wonderful person and Bill was very happy with her, but his parents did their best to run her off. They were openly critical of her, attacking her on their every visit. Bill's parents reproved her for her choice of jobs, passed judgment on her attire, and questioned her motives in dating their son. Even with all this pressure, Bill and Sue continued their relationship.

When their efforts to get rid of Sue didn't bring about the desired result, Bill's parents tried a new approach. They put pressure on Bill to allow them to continue their involvement in the couple's life. They were willing to put up with the new girlfriend so long as they could retain their hold on their son.

When Bill and Sue became engaged, the stakes became even more desperate for Bill's parents. Sue tried to be long-suffering, but it became clear that a caring and soft approach wouldn't be effective against the tenacity of Bill's parents. Finally Sue set a limit. She told Bill that if he wanted to continue this intrusive life-style with his parents, he would have to do it without her. She could go no further.

Painfully Bill made his choice. He wanted to be a good son, but he could see it was going to be difficult to be a good son *and* a good husband. He carefully weighed his options and decided that he loved Sue enough to risk his relationship with his parents.

After several false starts, he finally made it clear to his parents that things between him and them would have to be different. He asked for less contact and no drop-in visits. He had the locks changed on his house and didn't give them a new key. He told them that they would have to learn to accept his choices or he would have less to do with them. He refused to listen to their reprimands on the telephone and would hang up if their verbal onslaughts continued.

Bill's parents fought to avoid these changes. They attacked Sue, saying that it was she who had put Bill up to saying these cruel things

Just Say, "No"

to them. They weren't willing to accept the new relationship and evidently couldn't see how intrusively they were behaving.

After the wedding, Bill and Sue eventually chose to cut ties with his parents. He took a job several states away, seeking to find the autonomy he desired. His decision to move further away from his family was interesting, since his younger sister had also moved several states away, though in a different direction.

This example is extreme. Most of the time new boundaries won't be so vehemently fought. Others may not like your new limits, but they usually wouldn't go to such great lengths to oppose them. This example is included for two reasons. First, this story points out that even under the worst of circumstances, establishing new boundaries is possible. Second, while Bill went through a substantial level of discomfort to establish his new limits, he didn't die in the process. He fought for his new boundaries and although the outcome wasn't as happy as he would have wished, he was able to make choices which brought him a more desirable outcome. He was able to reclaim his power to choose.

POWER TO CHOOSE: What boundaries do you need to set in order to improve the quality of your life and/or relationships?

_____
_____
_____
_____
_____

4

SPEAKING UP IN RELATIONSHIPS
Reclaiming Your Power to Choose with Loved Ones

LLOYD CRAMER WAS DEPRESSED. He felt used and taken advantage of. He felt cheated out of the best life had to offer. He used that "P" word when describing his life—he felt like a pawn.

He described his plight like this. He said he felt like a person on the outside of a car with his hand on the handle of the door. When the car wasn't moving, life was uncomfortable. When the car was in motion, life seemed unbearable. He found himself being bumped and bashed as he bounced down the pavement. No matter how fast he ran, he could never run fast enough to avoid being hurt. He was bruised and bloodied every day just trying to keep up.

However, as much as he hurt, and as tired as he was of his bumpy ride, it never occurred to Lloyd that he could do something to change the direction of his life. His overriding wish, expressed in many ways and on frequent occasions, was that someone would get him loose! It hadn't dawned on him that *he* could take charge of his life and make some changes. He had robbed himself of his ***personal power to choose***.

Lloyd felt miserable, hurt and frustrated. His story was indeed sad. If he'd told others about his situation, they would no doubt have found his story lamentable. But he didn't tell anyone. That was part of the trap: to be miserable, but to keep it all a secret.

Lloyd had given away most of his choices by the time he was eleven. In his family it wasn't safe to be different. In fact it was so risky to disagree with their dad that he and his siblings found it easier to give in. It just wasn't worth the hassle to speak your mind.

He gave up more of his choices when he married. In his estimation, the marriage had been bad from the start. His relationship hadn't turned out to be anything like what he thought it would be. He believed that his wife, Elaine, had told him what she wanted him to believe and shown him what she wanted him to see in order to get him to the altar. In other words, he felt he'd been deceived.

When he and his wife had dated, they'd spent hours talking. Sometimes they were even late coming home from a date because they'd become so engrossed in a conversation that they lost track of time. They dated for seven months and were engaged for eight months and this penchant for talking continued throughout most of that time. Lloyd didn't realize it until after they were married, but when he looked back, it was clear that their conversations ended about a month and a half before the wedding.

They shared a number of activities before they married. They often played golf together. As a couple they attended movies, parties and plays. During this entire time, they got along well. There had seldom been a significant argument, except during the last two months before the wedding. The only disagreements that he remembered had been about the extent of their sexual involvement. They both wanted to "go further" than they had, but they also wanted to wait until after they were married. Lloyd had interpreted this to mean that his fiancee's desire for sexual involvement was as forceful as his. He was again sadly mistaken once they married.

As the time for the wedding neared, Lloyd had questions about whether or not to go through with the ceremony. He and Elaine had been tense and argumentative for several weeks before the wedding. Lloyd learned after they were married that Elaine, too, had considered delaying their marriage. However, neither of them had wanted to take the initiative to bring up the issues and discuss them or to delay or cancel the wedding altogether. They went ahead with the ceremony.

Even from the first week, Lloyd concluded that he'd made a terrible mistake and that they shouldn't have married. They argued about many issues. She thought he spent too much time with his friends. He thought she was too close to her mother. They snipped at each other over little things, like leaving their clothes lying around or who left the drinking glasses in the den. Their sex life suffered.

Their long talks were history. It was only now that Lloyd realized that they'd stopped talking before they married. Now instead of talking things through, they would have ridiculous fights over the smallest of offenses. These arguments just solidified his conviction that, "I never should have married her." Each disagreement was further evidence that their marriage was never going to work. After 15 years of saying to himself, "I made a terrible mistake and there's no way out!" Lloyd was convinced that life could never be any different.

But things changed for him. One day he allowed himself to accept the fact that he could in fact end the marriage. He could divorce. He didn't have to live like this. What a sigh of relief he breathed when that realization finally came to him! "I am not stuck here! I can get out!" And he decided that he would.

It was at that point that a strange thing happened. Soon after he realized that he could end the marriage, he also saw that he could stay in the marriage. For years he'd felt trapped in a difficult marriage. Now that he gave himself permission to get out, he realized that he didn't want to. He wanted to stay and make it work. To that end he and Elaine finally went to a marriage counselor and with hard work were able to heal their broken relationship. But the important point to consider at this stage in our discussion is this: the road to healing began with the realization that he could say, "No!"

If you don't believe that you have the freedom to say no to a relationship, saying yes isn't an act of freedom, but of compulsion. There is no real choice. Having to say yes is like going to the polls to vote, but having only one candidate on the ballot. There is no choice, although such staged elections may give the illusion of providing alternatives.

Finding a Path Out

The process of change isn't easy. There's no magic formula that I know of for bliss and happiness. I don't have the secret for marital ecstasy. Attempts which you make to change things are often faulty and faltering. Many avenues that you'll think can lead to change will turn out to be dead end streets. However, with perseverance, many unsatisfying marital situations can be altered.

Lloyd went through a helpful process as he began to take responsibility for his frustration and to recognize his power to choose. He made his **What Do I Stand to Lose?** list. The making of this list is an essential step toward regaining your power to choose. His list looked like the one on the next page.

Many people have explained to me how the making of this list was an essential step in freeing themselves so that they might regain their power to chose. Jayne suspected that her husband was involved with another woman. His constant absence from home, the countless business meetings, his secretiveness, his belligerent attitude, and his lack of interest in a sexual relationship with her all pointed in the

> **What Do I Stand To Lose
> If I Confront Elaine With My Complaints?**
> - Elaine might not take my issues seriously.
> - She might choose to attack or criticize me.
> - She might not want to pursue change.
> - There are times when Elaine and I are somewhat close. If I "rock the boat," we might lose the little closeness we do share.
> - We do make love occasionally. If I bring up my store of resentments and request lasting change, we might not make love at all.
> - Elaine might leave me.
> - If we do divorce, I would have a tough time with my religious conviction that marriage is forever.
> - I might lose the approval of my family if my marriage fails.
> - Can I make it on my own: emotionally, spiritually and financially?

direction of an affair. If she challenged him, he might leave. Could she live on her own? Only when she made a list of what she stood to lose and realized that she might not live as well, but that she would live, did she choose to confront him.

The next thing Lloyd did was insist that things be different with Elaine. That doesn't mean that he stood on the furniture, shaking his fist and making demands. He explained to her as calmly as possible the problems as he perceived them. He went on to explain that he wasn't content to continue living as they had. Having made his list, he knew he could live with what he might lose, so he talked straight to his wife. He wasn't ugly, but he was firm.

He went a step further with Elaine. He explained to her that he wasn't willing to continue talking to her alone about their problems. He wanted to involve a third party who could help them make changes. He thought they needed to have an objective listener. This turned out to be a valuable step. They were each able to be heard in their sessions. Their unbiased listener would then help them both get more of what they wanted. In counseling Lloyd and Elaine learned more about their power to chose. Lloyd began to take more responsibility for his own choices and their consequences.

The next step in the process looked like the end of the marriage, but it was the final step in the process of rebuilding it. While being involved in counseling improved many things, it didn't appear to

Lloyd that the situation was going to be different enough for him to want to continue in the marriage. It was at this point that he initiated a separation. He brought up his desire to move out during one the joint sessions with his wife at my office. When he moved out, I really didn't expect him to ever look back. He told me later that when he moved out in March, he firmly believed that he would be a free man, a single man, by Christmas. "What a present that would be for myself!" he'd thought.

Once he was out of the house, a strange thing happened. He found that once again when he was free to say no, he could choose to say yes. After years of wrestling with his uncertainty about being in the marriage, the separation allowed him the latitude to make a choice for which he could take responsibility. When he was no longer violating the principles of good choice-making, he found that he no longer felt trapped.

During the separation, Lloyd and Elaine continued their individual counseling sessions. There came a point when they wanted to discuss the possibilities of engaging in some dating behavior. They negotiated some time to talk, to go to movies and eventually discussed the renewal of their sexual relationship. This was a particularly risky step since so many of their arguments had been about their physical relationship.

They continued to grow during their time apart. As they dated, some of the old feelings of warmth were rekindled between them. After six months of being separated, they got back together. They'd been married for more than fifteen years, but they'd never felt as connected as they did when they were reunited. In the past Lloyd had felt trapped, but now, with the possibility of choices in front of him, he was choosing to be in this marriage.

This story could be repeated many times over. When couples regain their power to choose, it's amazing what it can do for their relationships! No longer do they have to settle for something less than what they wanted when they married. As they rediscover their power to choose, they're able to have that satisfying relationship that has eluded them.

Speaking Up is Important!

Unexpressed feelings and desires set up blockages, interrupting the healthy flow of energy into, through, and out of your reserve tank. In addition, storing old, negative feelings is a constant energy drain.

Unexpressed feelings also inhibit the flow of positive energy into the tank.

Have you ever had the experience of expressing something you'd been holding in and felt a tremendous sense of relief afterward? You may even have said, "That's a load off my chest!" You might have responded with, "I feel like a great, heavy burden has been lifted." When you open up, you might find yourself saying, "That's a load off my mind!" Such phrases indicate the sense of comfort that can follow your being honest.

Unexpressed feelings demand attention. When you ignore this demand, you'll always pay a price. Inhibiting your expression of feelings hurts you in two ways. First, it will hinder your growth as an individual. You won't be free to feel and express your emotions. You remain out of touch with yourself. The result is a passionless life.

Second, inhibiting your expression of feelings will hinder the health and growth of your relationships. All these things that you think you can't say will be stockpiled. The emotional and perhaps physical distance between you and your partner will increase. You'll find yourself saying tacky things and using cutting phrases. You can see how damaging this could be to living a healthy, whole life.

Why Didn't I Speak Up?

You may ask yourself, "Why didn't I speak up? Why didn't I tell him how I felt?" That's an important question, and one that requires attention. In fact I raised that very question with a group of several couples during a weekend retreat. Some of their responses were—

> "My issue is too petty to bring up." (Even though it has persisted for weeks or years.)
> "Maybe if I ignore how I feel, it will go away."
> "I don't want to be a nag!"
> "I don't want it to look like I want to be in control."
> "She might be angry with me."
> "He might reject me."
> "I'm not yet convinced that I have to express my feelings in order to be a whole person and/or for our relationship to be all it can be. If I don't have to, I certainly don't want to stir this stuff up!"

If you look closely at these objections and hesitancies, you'll see that they can be summed up in the following phrase:

If I tell you how I am really feeling, something bad will happen—one of us will be hurt or disappointed, you'll reject me, or you'll leave me.

As is the case with most self-protective rules, this axiom is self-defeating. Such reasoning will keep you caught in a bind. The only way to have a quality life is to work through anything that troubles you, and the only way to work through your issues is to confront them. Yet this rule prohibits your doing so. The end result is a stuckness that feels demoralizing. Your energy level falls because you don't feel the fulfillment of speaking up for yourself.

"We Need to Talk!"

Ursela was married to a man who used marijuana regularly. Whenever she complained about his drug use, Dexter would assure her that it didn't affect him. He said he only smoked so he could relax. Yes, it was illegal, but he was cautious and was certain he wouldn't get caught. When she complained because he stayed out until two in the morning running the streets, he said that she was asleep and she wouldn't miss him anyway. If she asked where all his money went, because he seldom seemed to have enough to cover his bills, he told her that he had expenses she didn't know about and that she would have to trust him.

Dexter made a good living as a manager of a sales team. He held down a responsible position and did well at work, earning his quarterly bonuses with regularity. Yet he couldn't come up with his share of the rent, couldn't cover his part of the utilities and often borrowed money from Ursela to pay for lunch for himself and gas for his car. When he left for his late night excursions, he most often took her car since it was nicer and usually had a full tank of gas.

To make her situation worse, Ursela described Dexter as critical and argumentative. Their discussions were seldom productive. They didn't focus on understanding each other and finding new alternatives. Their problem-solving sessions ended with Dexter putting her down, telling her their problems were her fault. If she would only be a better wife, he told her repeatedly, he would want to stay home. In fact, he even made her responsible for his drug use. He used, he said, because he had to chill out from the demands she put on him.

If You Can't Say No You Can't Really Say Yes

Ursela came to see that his behavior was unacceptable. She realized that she didn't have to live with his drug abuse and requested change. She strengthened her limits, saying that his being out until the early morning hours wasn't acceptable. Dexter made some minor changes, but their marriage remained much the same.

Even though Ursela had spoken up, she had a hard time expressing to Dexter exactly what she wanted. She balked at being honest and pointed about what she wanted. She was hesitant to regain her power of choice. At one of her sessions about six months into therapy, her counselor asked her to describe her marriage. Once again, Ursela gave the description you've just read. Her counselor asked what advantage she was receiving from her marriage, and Ursela couldn't name a thing. She was parenting alone, sleeping alone and paying the household expenses herself. Still she remained in the marriage. The counselor wondered aloud what it was that made her stay. With only a little thought, Ursela was able to answer with several compelling reasons.

- Perhaps he still doesn't understand me. If I could just find the right way to tell him what I don't like, maybe he'll change.
- I'm no saint myself. I've been ugly and hard to live with some times. I can't give up on Dexter when I know I'm imperfect.
- If I ever admit I might want to leave him, I'll have to admit I made a mistake.
- I've had a dream of having an intact family. If I pointedly communicate to Dexter what I want and he doesn't respond by changing, he might leave or I might want to leave, killing my dream.

These reasons to stay were so compelling that Ursela found it difficult to say no to Dexter. "No, you can't bring drugs into this house." "No, it isn't acceptable for you to be out with friends until two in the morning." "No, when you yell at me and call me names, I am not in the mood for anything romantic." Only when she was able to say no, only then would she feel the strength of her power to choose.

POWER TO CHOOSE: What do you need to say to someone in your world that you've been afraid or hesitant to say?

How can you speak up? How can you most effectively tell others what you want and how you feel? In the following chapter, we will spend time examining the structure of your communication.

5

WE NEED TO TALK!
Communicating What You Need From Others

IF YOU CAN'T COMMUNICATE effectively, you can't regain your choices. Only when you're able to express yourself effectively to the people in your world can you hope to exercise your power to choose.

Consider the case of Mark and Lisa. Mark has a problem. He doesn't know it yet, but he has a problem. Mark thinks it's his job to protect his wife, Lisa, from the criticism she receives from her mother. He believes he's helping Lisa, but helping isn't the word she has used to describe what he does.

The latest example occurred last Saturday while he and Lisa were visiting at his in-laws' home. Lisa's mother began to criticize her for continuing her career and leaving their two-year-old son in day care. As Lisa was calmly explaining her point of view to her mother, Mark stepped in. In loud and angry tones he told his mother-in-law that she was living in the past. He encouraged her to take a look around to see how much things had changed since the '50s. Mark felt a sense of satisfaction at having "helped" his wife. Meanwhile, Lisa looked on in shock.

Later, as they drove home from their visit, Lisa said she wanted to talk about the conversation with her mother. Mark expected Lisa to

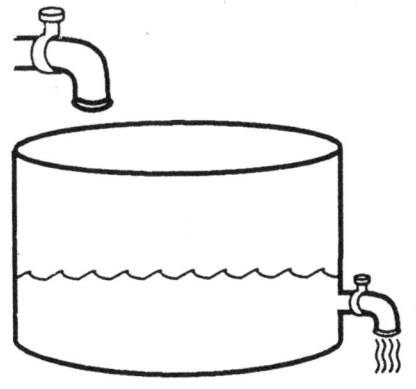

Despite good intentions, her tank is depleted by his attempts to help.

thank him for rescuing her from her mother's onslaught. Instead, she told him how angry she was that he'd interfered. Mark couldn't believe it! How could she criticize him for only wanting to help?

Anatomy of Your Communication

Communication is a complicated process. If you're to communicate effectively with others, there are several facets of the process that you'll need to keep in mind. First, remember an axiom in communication theory which states:

You cannot *not* communicate.

Even when you say *nothing,* you communicate *something.* In fact, silence is often the most profound form of communication. Many spouses and lovers have complained when their partners don't talk to them. The silence they experience communicates a strong message to them. A woman will often ask her mate, "What's wrong? Why are you so quiet?" Silence says something.

If someone you know walks up to you and says, "Hi! How are you?" and you turn and walk away without saying a word, you'll have said nothing but communicated volumes. Exactly what you've communicated will have to be interpreted by the other person, but you've communicated a great deal without uttering a word.

Second, most of what you communicate you'll communicate nonverbally. You may take care to say the correct words and that attention to the words you speak is valuable. However, there's much more that you express to others apart from your words.

Experts have broken down the process of communicating into these proportions:
- 7% verbal
- 38% tone of voice
- 55% body language and nonverbal cues

These percentages and their differing weights emphasize the need to give attention to the total message you're communicating. Did you notice that 93% of your communication is non-verbal? The overwhelming majority of what you communicate is communicated with messages other than your words themselves!

If a husband says to his wife, "You sure did a good job!" in a gruff, sarcastic voice, the verbal message will probably be lost in the nonverbal. When asked later what he said, the husband may report that he told his wife she did well, while the wife's recollection will no doubt be much different. Learning to recognize and becoming willing to address incongruity in the verbal and nonverbal messages is essential to effective communication.

Third, it will be important to note the "report" and "command" aspects of communication. The report portion of your message is what you actually said. "Get off the phone!" may be a description of what was said in a conversation. The command segment of the communication involves what's implied about the relationship between the speaker and the hearer. "Get off the phone!" when shouted by an irritated father to his daughter who has been on the telephone for 45 minutes implies a relationship in which one has the authority to make a demand and expect the other to comply. Those same words spoken to his wife in a similar tone would imply a heirarchical relationship with which most wives would be uncomfortable.

The Cycle of Communication

Discussing an issue is a complex undertaking. An issue is anything which needs to be addressed. The issue could be something that has come up now for the first time or it could be a sensitive or volatile area that has been hashed and rehashed. Regardless of the intensity of the issue, there are always five aspects of the discussion which must be present if you're to communicate effectively. The model could be described like this:

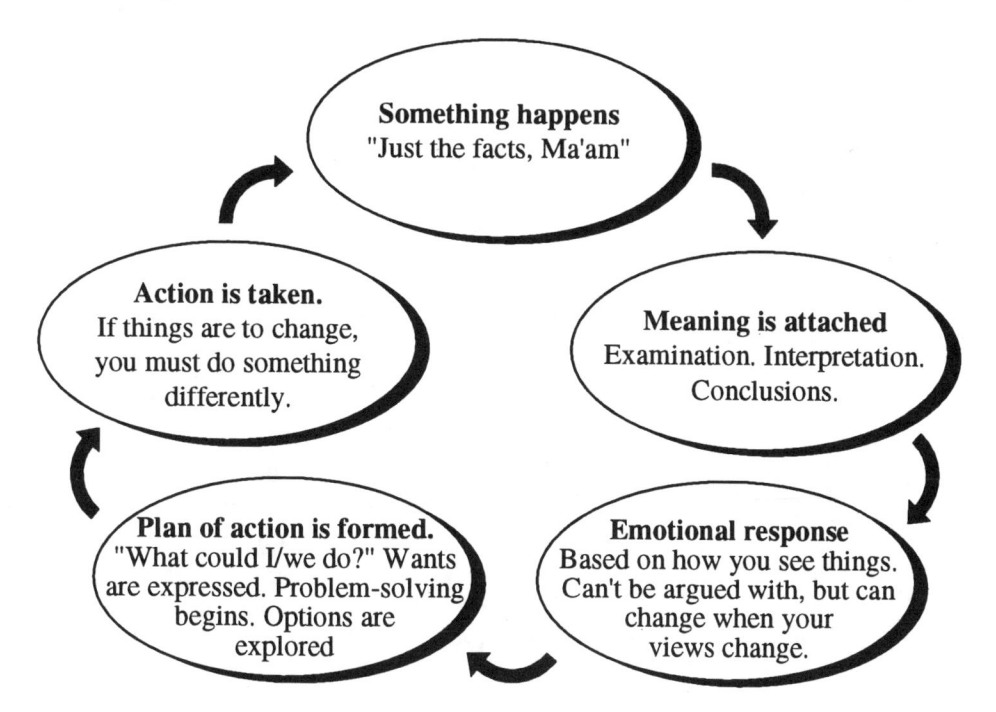

Something happens
"Just the facts, Ma'am"

Meaning is attached
Examination. Interpretation. Conclusions.

Emotional response
Based on how you see things. Can't be argued with, but can change when your views change.

Plan of action is formed.
"What could I/we do?" Wants are expressed. Problem-solving begins. Options are explored

Action is taken.
If things are to change, you must do something differently.

In the process of communicating about an issue, it will be necessary to give attention to all five of these areas. Because this information is so important, each segment of the cycle will be discussed separately. You'll learn how better to communicate what you want, how to listen to the other person and how to problem-solve so that both of you can get what you want.

Something happens. Like Sgt. Joe Friday in the *Dragnet* series, at this point you want only to recall the facts. This step is the foundation for all the others. Remember: no two people will view what happened in exactly the same way. Still, it's important to discuss your own recollection of the facts because your view will have affected how you've responded. Facts would include movement from here to there, time of day, the words that were said, who was standing where, etc.

Meaning is attached. When things happen, you have a built-in need to make sense of them. In order to accomplish this, you examine what has happened in order to draw conclusions. Your meanings are subject to fallibility and should be held tentatively. They might be best thought of as being set in firm Jell-O®. Your interpretations are subject to change when more information is gathered or when you change the way you perceive the information you have before you. Examples of interpretations would be: "It's hot in here." "You're late!" "That was an insensitive thing to do." "You're always telling me what to do!"

Emotional response. Your emotions just are. They can't be discounted or argued with. Even if you don't like the way you feel, you have to accept how you feel before you can make any kind of effective changes. Since your emotions are based on your view of what has happened, your feelings can only change when your interpretations change. There are a wide range of human emotions. You cheat yourself if you restrict yourself to feeling or expressing only a few.

Plan of action is formed. Based on what has happened, the meaning you have attached and your emotional response, you become aware of something that you want to be different. In order to begin the process of problem-solving, each person involved in solving the issue will need to express his or her wants and needs. Expressing a desire doesn't mean you'll automatically get what you desire, but expressing your wants is a vital step. Suggestions could be made as to what might be done differently. Brainstorming could be used to generate choices. In the course of discussing the issue, the meaning you've attached to what happened may change. Your feelings may then change.

Action is taken. Something must be done differently if things are to change. If all two people ever do is talk about their problems without doing something in a new or alternative way, they'll probably feel frustrated. Things in a relationship change when something is done differently.

Applying the Cycle

Let's go back now to the problem that Mark had with Lisa. He believes he's being helpful when he speaks up for Lisa when she argues with her mother. However, Lisa's reaction to him when he does this is anything but appreciative. He has concluded that she's either a very unthankful person or he's doing something she doesn't appreciate. He decides to talk to her.

First, he makes an appointment to talk to Lisa when neither of them is tired or emotionally agitated. Attempts at problem-solving in the middle of a heated argument are almost always futile. In as calm, but firm a way as possible, Mark shares his view with his wife. He wonders why she reacts so coldly to his attempts to help her.

Lisa has a viewpoint of her own. She tells him that she sees his attempts at helping her as an implication that she isn't capable of handling the situation herself. She feels put down and angry when he treats her in a way that she perceives implies that she's fragile or inept.

Mark was shocked to hear Lisa's side of the issue. He'd always assumed that his attempts to block his mother-in-law's criticisms were a way to show his love for his wife. He'd intended to help her, to shield her, so to speak. He didn't realize he was in fact offending her.

After hearing how Lisa view his actions, Mark apologized. Vowing to be helpful in differing ways, he asked her what he could do. Lisa suggested that if Mark really wanted to affirm her, he could do so with a wink at her from across the room or give her a thumbs up when she and her mother were arguing. In this way she would know of his support, but wouldn't sense the interference of his previous attempts to help.

They put this plan into effect. They set a time to check back with each other as to the effectiveness of this solution after an upcoming trip to visit her parents.

If You Can't Say No You Can't Really Say Yes

Things won't always turn out as well as this when discussions occur around an issue. Hurt feelings and years of accumulated resentments often get in the way of beneficial discussions. Lisa might have had some trust issues to work through with Mark. Can she trust him now? Will he follow through? Mark might have been angry that Lisa didn't speak up before now and tell him how she felt. Why didn't she tell him long ago? Often issues can become quite complicated.

These additional issues are handled just like the initial issue. Each one is discussed. Only when each partner speaks up with his or her side of things can the situation change.

Finding Missing Pieces

There are times when something that *hasn't* been said will take away your personal power. If you're the one who hasn't spoken up, you may feel a need to hold back. You can't be yourself. You have to pretend the current situation is different than it is. You may bring up something to discuss that's more a distraction than the real issue. Your personal power can be reclaimed only when your communication becomes honest. You have to say what you really feel or what you want in order for things to change. The only avenue to true intimacy is through honest, shared communication in which each person makes it clear what he or she wants and feels and perceives that it's understood by the other person. People who communicate with such honesty get more out of life and experience a higher level in their emotional reserve tanks.

Your tank rises to a higher level as your needs are met.

Couples often have sizable arguments because some parts of their communication are missing. For instance, one wife, Michelle, who's been a rather traditional wife for the ten years she's been married, hesitatingly asks her husband, Jack, if it would be all right if she went out one night a week with two of her women friends. Jack's been thinking, but hasn't said, that he fears he and Michelle have been drifting apart lately. When she makes her request, he thinks of it as further evidence of the growing distance between them. However, he still doesn't speak up about his concerns. In effect, he gives up his personal power by discussing other issues.

Jack could have answered Michelle's proposal with a discussion of his concerns, but he didn't do so. He could have said, "I have no problem with your going out once a week as long as it's as simple as that." Then he and his wife could have had a different conversation. Instead, he first asks her why she can't just talk to her friends on the telephone. Then he tells her, "It would be dangerous for you to be out at night." When it becomes clear that his "reasoning" isn't dissuading her, Jack puts his foot down. "Well, you're married to me and you should stay at home in the evenings and make dinner." As you can imagine, the tension rises in their conversation as each of these distractions are offered as the reason for his rejecting her proposal.

This type of discussion may be an all-too-familiar scenario for you. Do you find yourself arguing with others over small issues? Do you seem to spend a tremendous amount of energy discussing things that don't really seem to be the issue? How can you change things?

The bottom line answer to truly changing your communication is *risk*. It's risky to say what you want and need. Why is Michelle asking for what she wants in such a tentative way? What keeps Jack from bringing up the issue that disturbs him? It happens because they're afraid to risk. Suppose Jack did say that he was concerned about the increasing distance he'd felt. To do so would be to take a chance, even though it could open the door for meaningful communication. Michelle might disagree, she might attack him verbally, or he might be fearful of appearing needy. To express yourself honestly is to take a risk.

If Michelle spoke up directly and asked for what she needed, Jack might see it as her drawing battle lines. They both might wind up in a defensive stance. If Jack explained his concern, Michelle might minimize his issue or criticize him for being honest. Healthy communication demands a commitment to the risk of honesty.

Many husbands and wives have had the fruitless kind of arguments that Michelle and Jack experienced. Matt and his wife had one recently. They argued because some very important things were being left unsaid. Matt's perspective was that Sharon had been sexually unavailable lately. Even when they were together, she seemed to be somewhere else. Matt had stored up growing feelings of frustration for some time rather than confronting them as he became aware of them.

When he finally brought the issue up to his wife, Matt had saved up a long list of her sins. Initially he didn't even talk about the sexual issues. Instead, he told her he thought she was withdrawing from him. He told her that she didn't seem to care about him. He suggested that she wasn't working as hard in the marriage as he was. In order to bolster his case, Matt made several "always" and "never" statements. "You're never really here!" "You always pull away from me!" ("Always" and "never" statements are *always* lies and are *never* true!) The bottom line of his argument was that he was innocent and she was very guilty.

In the middle of the quarrel, he remembered thinking to himself, "*I* don't even believe what I'm saying!" But he hung firm, not wanting to give in. During a pause he and Sharon looked at each other, recognizing the hurt they were causing one another and the fruitlessness of their discussion.

There came a turning point in the argument. It was the reason they were able to back away from the logjam they'd created and were able to talk about what was really bothering them. They both stood there, eyes on fire. In that moment they caught a glimpse of what they were doing to themselves, each other, and their marriage. Matt wanted something more, something different. Sharon did, too. Since he'd brought up the issue initially, he decided to try again. This time he was more honest.

When Matt finally told Sharon what was bothering him, she began to cry. She told him that she hadn't felt much desire to be sexual with him because she felt he wasn't being sensitive to her needs. She'd gone to her parents' home two weeks before to be with her father during surgery. She told him that when she returned, her friends took a greater interest in how she was doing than he had. Since she perceived him to be unavailable for her, she hadn't felt close to him. Sex for her was more like going through the motions than an expression of intimacy.

All this was news to Matt. He thought he'd been supportive to a laudable degree. He hadn't complained when she left. He'd kept the house clean and organized while she was gone: cooking dinner, washing clothes, caring for the children. When she returned, he met her at the airport with a flower and a very warm kiss. Matt didn't understand how Sharon could say he hadn't been supportive.

As they continued to talk, they discovered that the bottom line was that Matt had supported her the way *he* might have wanted to be supported, but he hadn't supplied what she needed. And for her part, Sharon had been hesitant to ask for what she needed. Talking about what was missing opened the door to renewed closeness.

Differences in Communication Style

This incident from the life of Matt and Sharon points up the fact that there are differences in needs, which lead to differences in communication styles between men and women. An observer who watched men and women communicate might even conclude that they were speaking a different language altogether, or at least two very distant dialects.

Many studies and investigations have been done about the contrasts in the way the sexes converse. Some of the most common findings are summarized below:

- Women are more sensitive in perceiving the non-verbal communication cues of others than are men.
- Men invade other people's body space more often than do women.
- Men touch others more often than do women and tend to do so in more forceful ways.
- Men fidget and shift their body position more than do women.
- Women maintain more eye contact during positive communication than do men.
- Men maintain more eye contact during conflicted communication than do women.
- Men interrupt others more often, speak in louder tones and speak at a slower rate of speed than do women.
- Women disclose more personal information about themselves than do men.
- Women tend to frame confrontations and requests in softer language ("Honey, would you get another chair, please?") and use more tag endings than do men ("That's a pretty house, isn't it?")
- Women are more apt to use feeling words, use more terms of endearment, and show affection more openly than are men.

- Men tend to approach a problem analytically, while women tend to do so more emotionally.
- Women are more maintenance-oriented ("Does anyone need more potatoes or green beans?"), while men are more task-oriented ("What's our plan for tonight?")
- Women hold more grudges than do men.
- Men are more blunt than are women.
- Women are more likely to ask for help than are men, who try to figure things out on their own.

Let me summarize this list of differences with an illustration. This will be a bit oversimplified, but I believe it will make the point. Every human being has a hard side and a soft side. Your hard side is the part of you that makes plans, gets things done, organizes events, thinks through problems and takes a strong stand on issues. Your soft side is the part of you which senses your emotions, has compassion on others, is in touch with your intuitive self, takes into consideration the needs and desires of other people and allows you to truly connect with other people. In our culture, men are encouraged to honor and be more responsive to their hard side, while women are encouraged to respond to their soft side. If men and women are to have any chance at effective communication, they'll have to listen to both sides. Men will have to cultivate their soft side and women their hard side.

It's common for a man to simply say, "This is what I want!" without paying much attention to how it might affect the woman in his life. He's not necessarily being rude. He'd probably think of it as being direct. At the same time, it's not uncommon for a woman to hesitate to ask for what she wants. She may think that her husband or boyfriend should be as intuitive as she is. "He should know what I want without my having to ask." She may be slow to speak up because she doesn't want to appear pushy or demanding. This difference contains the pebble which can grow into a mountain of discord. Resolution is only possible if he responds more with his feeling side and she's able to ask for what she wants by responding to the side of herself which sets limits.

Suggestions for Resolving Conflicts

When you're ready to talk, when you want the conflict to be resolved in a more helpful way, here are some suggestions which can help.

- **Choose carefully a time to talk.** Have your discussion when both of you are rested. Limit distractions. Talk at a time when each of you can give your undivided attention. (Terrible times to talk: when the children are demanding attention or when one of you is watching a favorite television program.)
- **Discuss one issue at a time.** Don't get sidetracked. If your spouse is discussing her displeasure at your lack of support for her career, this wouldn't be a good time to discuss her forgetting to call you to tell you she was going to be late. If her being late without calling is an issue, make an appointment to discuss that at another time.
- **Set a time limit.** Thirty minutes is the maximum for most couples. After that, fatigue sets in. Personal attacks occur more often when you're tired and rehashing the argument becomes easier to do.
- **Speak in "I messages."** Avoid saying things like, "You're such a bitch!" Rather, own what you want to say. "I get angry when I have to make all the arrangements when we go out."
- **Listen to both your hard side and your soft side.** Remember that men and women communicate differently. If you're to communicate effectively, you'll have to be in touch with both sides of yourself.
- **Focus on the problem, not your partner.** Seek to answer the question, "What went wrong?" rather than "Who did something wrong?" A personal attack will most often result in defensiveness which makes it difficult to problem-solve.
- **Listen with both ears.** Read between the lines. Often the real issue hasn't yet been discussed. It may take some effort to identify other issues. Listen carefully. However, avoid scrutinizing every issue as if there's always something else to be discussed. This could lead to mind reading.
- **If your desire is to win, you'll both lose.** Seek a resolution that's fair to both of you. Stand your ground, but decide what's important to you. Listen to your partner and help him or her get what he/she wants, too.

Remember, if you're to exercise your power to choose, effective communication is essential. Every effort you make to improve the way you communicate will pay choice-making dividends.

If You Can't Say No You Can't Really Say Yes

POWER TO CHOOSE: One positive thing you could say about your communication skills is:

_____
_____
_____
_____
_____

PART TWO

CHALLENGING OLD MESSAGES

6

CAN YOU FEEL ANYTHING WHEN I DO THIS?
Reconnecting With Your Emotions

ON A TUESDAY IN FEBRUARY five years ago, life began to change forever for Arnold. That was the day he met Sarah Hanson.

Sarah opened a door and allowed him to peer into a new and exciting world that he'd imagined, but seldom visited. She showed him how to feel again. Arnold didn't know at the time that he wasn't feeling. All he was aware of was that something was missing in his life. When he could feel again, it was as if his eyes had been opened, perhaps for the first time in his life. It's the most rewarding gift anyone has ever given him. In a very real sense, she gave him back his life.

Arnold recently received word that Sarah had died. He cried spontaneously as he held the card from her husband that explained the circumstances of her death. It's not extraordinary that a person would cry upon receiving news of the death of someone who'd a great impact on him. However, since he'd been disconnected from his feelings for so long, the fact that he could cry was a tribute to the work she'd done with him.

Reconnecting with Feelings

Arnold met Sarah in Texas when he went for treatment due to depression. He went into this setting because he knew he needed help, but even when he arrived, he tried to keep looking good in front of all the other patients. The other patients even wondered why he was there. Looking good was the way he'd lived his life, so the role of appearing to be better than he felt wasn't difficult for him to take.

Sarah saw through it all. She could see his pain. Like a pit bull, she took after Arnold. He says he was angry and felt controlled by her at the time. Twenty eight days later he couldn't thank her enough.

Sarah seemed to know just where to touch him to get him to say, "Ouch!" One part of her gift was being able to come up with very effective homework tasks. Two or three days after he arrived, she gave him the first in a series of assignments designed to unbalance his carefully created world and get him back in touch with his feelings.

Arnold's first assignment was this: He was required to express how he felt before he could speak to anyone. One fellow patient told him later that the first thing Arnold said to her on her first day on the unit was, "I feel controlled and manipulated!" Before Arnold could order dinner in the cafeteria, he began with something like, "I feel hungry." If he wanted an aspirin from the nurse, he would begin with, "I feel stressed." Later Arnold said, "I can't explain to you how frustrating it is for a person who is out of touch with emotions to have to begin every communication with an 'I feel' statement. Everything in me wanted to rebel from doing this exercise!"

After this assignment, Arnold wasn't really feeling his emotions, but he was becoming aware of how disconnected from them he'd become. He'd become very adept at doing his emotions in his head. Like a disinterested third party, his intellect would report that his behavior *looked* like fear or anxiety, but he seldom *felt* fearful or anxious.

Sarah took things a step further. She had him spend an entire weekend saying only, "Yes" and, "No" to anyone who addressed him. This shut down his intellectualizing and talking as ways to avoid emotions. Arnold reported in his group meeting after the weekend that he felt as if he'd been living in a pressure cooker for the last three days.

Reconnection Begins

Arnold had come to treatment because he was clinically depressed. He was in a job that he hated, his marriage was coming apart, and he was having an affair with a woman he worked with. His emotional reserve tank was so empty it was all he could do to make it through the day. Every morning he had to pump himself up just to get to the office. Evenings at home were hell. The relationship with his co-worker that had been so exciting a few months before left him now in a pit of guilt and depression that seemed bottomless. He felt empty, depleted and tired.

All these emotions came in a flood as Arnold became still and quiet. There was an almost overwhelming sense of sadness that swept

Can You Feel Anything When I Do This?

Depleters:
-out of touch with emotions
-poor choices
-guilt

over him. He began to experience the power of his feelings for the first time in a long time.

But Sarah wasn't finished. The next weekend his task was to be totally silent from Friday afternoon until Monday morning. He wasn't to speak at all. He could sign, act or pantomime for what he wanted, but he wasn't to talk to anyone. Even dinner was chosen by pointing instead of ordering aloud. In addition, she stressed that it wouldn't be appropriate for him to isolate himself all weekend. She put him with people, but kept him in silence.

When the feelings began to surface, there was mostly a sense of sadness. Arnold grieved the childhood he never had because of his parents' expectations that their children should be little adults. Arnold recalled that he'd heard comments since he could remember about how he was "mature beyond his years." He'd long since forgotten how to let the child inside of him play.

After grief came anger. Lots of it. Anger over his lost childhood. Anger at the way he'd hurt himself, his friends and his family due to his inability to feel his own feelings and take responsibility for his own behavior. Anger at himself for believing the male lie taught to growing boys and repressed men in our culture: **It's *not* OK to feel!** Except anger. Express your anger and lot's of it. But don't be soft enough to hurt or be afraid.

Arnold took out his anger several times on a punching bag. After one of his sessions, he removed his gloves to find that all of his knuckles were bruised and bleeding. Three decades of built up frustration was finally coming out!

The final piece of the puzzle that Sarah provided for him came in the form of a psychodrama which she skillfully crafted. She asked him to wait outside the group therapy room while she described what she wanted from the other members of the group who were to be players in the drama.

When Arnold walked into the room, the positioning of the players left him with a cold, sinking feeling. He didn't know what was about to happen, but he knew immediately it was going to be emotional. His stomach fell to his knees.

The scene looked like this: four women were standing in a circle around a man with their hands around his throat. Each of them was gently but surely attempting to strangle him. Each of the women was saying something, but in the jumble of words, Arnold couldn't make out what they were saying. The man in the middle whose throat was covered by eight hands said over and over in a feeble voice, "Help! Help me! Help me, please!"

He looked to Sarah for an explanation. "This is your inner child, Arnold," she said. "The playful, spontaneous, fully spiritual part of you is being slowly murdered by the expectations you're trying to meet. Those expectations are coming from your parents, your career, your wife and your church. You're attempting with so much fervor to please them all that you've allowed that precious child inside of you to despair of life."

Sarah nodded and the women began to speak once again, this time one at a time. They voiced the expectations, the demands of each of the four parts of the world which were pulling at him. "You can do better than that!" "Can't you take care of this?" "Be sure to be home early!" "Be careful what you say in class on Sunday." "Don't rock the boat!" Throughout all this, the child in the middle continued to plead for help in his pitiful voice.

Arnold ached for this part of him that was so lost and in so much pain. He asked her what he needed to do. "Set him free!" Sarah said.

Without hesitation he started toward the four women. It was his plan to physically remove the hands that were choking his child. Sarah spoke up. "One rule. You can't touch them."

Arnold backed away. He looked at Sarah in confusion. His eyes asked for a hint as to what to do, but she left him to figure it out.

He tried yelling at them to stop. "Don't say that!" "Let him go!" "Can't you see what you're doing?" "No one could live up to those expectations!" But no one moved. He tried yelling even louder, but not one of them even seemed to notice. This wasn't going to work.

Then a new direction became clear to him. If he couldn't control them, he would have to strengthen that child. How could he nurture that kid in the middle? What could he do or say that could save him?

He would have to love him back into a sense of strength so he could set himself free. That was his plan!

Arnold began to talk fervently to that threatened child. "Don't listen to them. Take care of yourself. You can stop *doing* and just *live*. You deserve it! I love you and I'll take care of you. I'm sorry I ignored you for so long. Please hear me! Please trust me!"

Slowly the man in the middle broke away. One by one the hands around his neck fell away as the unreasonable expectations were left behind. When he was finally free, Arnold embraced him. With tears he welcomed him back. Arnold would say later than in all his life, he couldn't remember receiving a more meaningful hug!

Arnold will never be the same because of those experiences! A whole new world has been opened up to him—a world of feeling and intuition and gut level responses and passion! Five years later, Arnold confesses that with all his effort, he still only feels his emotions about half the time. It takes a long time for such a deeply ingrained pattern to change. But when he does feel his emotions, life seems more alive and fresh than he ever imagined.

The Vital Importance of Feelings

Identifying and expressing your feelings is crucial to the process of reclaiming your power to choose. Only when you know how you are being affected emotionally, physically and spiritually can you respond in an appropriate manner. To the degree that you're out of touch with these important, internal cues, to that extent will your personal power to choose be compromised. This is work you'll be compelled to do. There's no way around the work that leads to reconnecting with your feelings!

Your family background and your present experience may provide many prohibitions against feeling your emotions. Consider some of these commonly heard messages:

- "Don't cry or I'll give you something to cry about!"
- "Don't worry, it won't hurt!" (As in, "The doctor needs to give you a shot, but don't worry, it won't hurt!")
- "Take it like a man!"
- "Good girls don't talk like that!"
- "You don't *really* feel that way!"
- "Go to your room and stay there until you can put a smile on your face!"

It doesn't take a lot of investigation to uncover the fact that many men and women have become adept at masking over, covering up, lying about and stuffing their feelings. When someone asks you the question, "How do you feel?", you may have no clue how to answer. "Fine" is a common response, but, "Fine" isn't a feeling word. It's a word which communicates little or nothing about the emotional state of the person who's speaking.

When so much emphasis is placed on avoiding how you feel, you miss many important bits of information. You stay out of touch with the level of your reserve tank. And your options will be limited in situations which call for a decision or action because you know so little about yourself. You'll be guessing about what you need, like the driver of a car in which the gas gauge no longer works. "I think I've got enough fuel to make it," you may say, even up to the moment when you run out of gas.

Can't Argue With a Feeling

Feelings are neither good nor bad. They just are. How you feel can't be argued with or denied without negative consequences. Even if you don't like the way you feel, you must give yourself permission to feel the way you feel if you're to have any success in changing the way you feel.

No matter how hostile, frantic, or anxiety-provoking your feelings may be, you must accept the fact that your feelings exist if you're to reclaim your personal power. Nothing will empty your tank more quickly than denying, stuffing or living life unaware of your emotions.

Let me illustrate what it's like to deny your feelings by comparing it to traveling on a highway. Interstate 40 runs across Tennessee from Memphis in the West to Knoxville in the East. In the center of the state on this highway is Nashville. Let's suppose you were in Nashville and you wanted to go west to Memphis. You could get on the interstate and travel directly to that destination. Now suppose that once you're on I-40, the little green roadsigns on the side of the highway indicate that you're getting closer to Knoxville instead of closer to Memphis. Something is wrong. You're going the wrong direction! What do you need to do? The response that makes the most sense is to stop, take a look at where you are and make the changes which are appropriate to get to Memphis.

If you handled going the wrong way on the highway in the same manner that you often handle your feelings, you would just deny you're going the wrong way. "Me? I'm not lost. I know where I'm going." "Who says Memphis is in that direction?" "Sign? What sign?" Only when you admit *where you are* and *where you're headed* can you take the steps necessary to get *where you want to be.*

You have to handle your feelings in the same way. If you're anxious, but don't want to be anxious, you must first admit your anxiety before you can begin the process of change. Denying, minimizing, rationalizing or blaming will keep you stuck in the emotion you don't want to feel. However, when you allow yourself to *feel,* then you can get back on the road to where you want to be.

Most men and women I know who try to acknowledge their feelings at all tend to treat them like a scientific experiment. They distance themselves from the passion of their feelings by being an only-slightly-interested-from-a-great-distance third party. Your emotions can't be handled that way.

In order to be emotional, you'll have to be willing to get dirty. Some feelings can be handled at arm's length so that no residue gets on you. Others have to be embraced or even wrestled with. You'll have stuff all over yourself before you're done with a feeling like remorse or frustration!

Emotions will clamor for attention even if you ignore them. Anger unexpressed doesn't dissipate. Instead, it seeps underground, becoming frustration, resentment or depression instead. In addition, it takes a tremendous amount of reserve tank energy to stuff a powerful feeling like anger! Fear, when unexpressed, accumulates and can take the form of a sense of dread. Anxiety that's not acted upon may show up in the form of physical symptoms like headaches, ulcers or panic attacks.

Getting back in touch with feelings is some of the most demanding work any person will ever attempt. Arnold's example at the beginning of this chapter attests to that fact. Reconnecting with emotions that have been long repressed or learning to listen again to the feelings that are speaking to you will be a challenge like none other you've ever undertaken. It's dirty, painful work. Family secrets and past hurts will have to be admitted and explored. There isn't a short-cut.

However, it's also the most rewarding work you'll ever do. To feel again is like hearing after your ears have been clogged due to a cold or infection. It's like being able to see again after being in pitch black darkness. To actually feel your emotions in your body affirms your humanness. You can sense your power to act when you feel your anxiety or your current and helpful anger building up inside.

Change won't come quickly. You can't immediately unlearn a denial pattern you've been living with for thirty or forty or fifty years. But change can happen.

Feelings Come in All Shapes and Sizes

There are a wide variety of feelings, in all sorts of shades, shapes and degrees. It has been suggested that the hundreds of varied emotions can be placed into four main categories: mad, glad, sad, and afraid. Some feelings which fall into these four categories would include:

MAD	**GLAD**	**SAD**	**AFRAID**
annoyed	buoyant	disappointed	alarmed
belligerent	carefree	discontented	anxious
bitter	cheerful	discouraged	apprehensive
cross	contented	down	dismayed
angry	joyful	hurt	scared
enraged	ecstatic	gloomy	fearful
furious	elated	heavy-hearted	frightened
grumpy	excited	low	hysterical
irritated	exhilarated	somber	insecure
offended	inspired	sullen	nervous
pissed	satisfied	unhappy	terrified
resentful	serene	worthless	worried

The more of these feelings you give yourself permission to experience, the more of life you'll consciously perceive. If you only have permission to express one or two, you'll be very limited in the way you react to your world. Things will look mostly black and white. If you can only be angry or numb, where does scared fit in? If you can't express anxiety, it may come out as anger instead. On the other hand, if you have given yourself permission to express a wide range of emotions, you'll be much less restricted.

If you're attempting to sort an array of colors into only two categories, black and white, many of your choices will be difficult and your final categories may not be of much use. Yellow would be nearer white than black. Violet would be nearer black than white. Where would a vivid green fit? How about light blue? Having only two choices makes categorization difficult and the final product may not be very usable.

However, if you had four categories, such as red, yellow, blue and black, the job of assigning colors is easier and the outcome is more helpful. If there are a dozen categories, the end result would be even more functional. So it is with your feelings. The more emotions you can feel, the more you'll benefit from the feedback they provide.

Feelings Travel in Triads

How do your feelings develop? Is there a direct connection between what happens and how you feel? If your child spills his milk, is your emotional response automatic? If someone criticizes you, do you have any power over how you feel?

Feelings don't exist in isolation. Your feelings always travel in a triad. You'll remember from the discussion in Chapter 5 that there are three distinct parts which result in a particular feeling:

Something happens ⇨ Meaning is attached ⇨ Emotional response

Something happens. These are only the facts. Facts would include movement from here to there, time of day, the words that were said, who was standing where, etc.

Meaning is attached. Attaching meaning is your attempt to make sense out of your world. You interpret what happens to you and around you. You're constantly attaching meaning even if you're unaware that you're doing it. Your meanings are subject to fallibility and should be held tentatively. Your interpretations are subject to change when more information is gathered or when you change the way you perceive the information you have before you. Examples of interpretations would be: "You don't love me!", "You expect too much from me!" and "You're always trying to control me!"

Emotional response. Remember, your emotions just are. They can't be discounted or argued with. Even if you don't like the way you feel, you have to accept how you feel before you can make any kind of effective change. Since your emotions are based on your view of what has happened, your feelings can change when your interpretations change.

The fact that your emotions grow out of your interpretations means that *you alone are responsible for your feelings*. No one else is to blame. It's not appropriate to say, "You made me angry!" When you're exercising your personal power to choose, you know that no one has the right or the power to make you feel any particular way. You'll take responsibility for your own feelings and let others do the same with theirs. When you can do this, when you can own your feelings and detach from the feelings of other people, then your feelings can be used to guide you toward the serenity you're seeking in life.

If your goal is to enhance the quality of your life, your interpretations will have to be challenged. If you take bad drivers or slow traffic personally, you'll be angry and upset in a traffic jam. If you can change your interpretation, you can find yourself being less keyed up in traffic. If you interpret every, "No!" from your two-year-old as a challenge to your authority, your emotional response will be much different than if you see his use of, "No!" as a way to discover the limits of his world.

You may hold some beliefs that color your interpretations and lead to emotional responses you'd rather avoid. Some examples of such beliefs would include:

- I must be treated fairly in all situations!
- Everyone should like me.
- My performance must always go well.
- If I receive any criticism, I have failed.

If you're to change your outcomes so that you experience your feelings in a useful and meaningful fashion, such demanding and unreasonable beliefs will have to be challenged and altered.

Feelings and Hindered Choices

If you want to live life to the full, you can't ignore your feelings. Although your feelings aren't the focal point of your existence, they are a barometer of what's going on in your life.

Your feelings are an indicator of the condition of your inner life and your reactions to your world. When you want to know, "What's happening with me?" your feelings reflect the answer. But you must listen. If you don't plug in to your emotions, much of the richness of life will elude you.

Julia has been married for 17 years to Tom. Overall she's been happy with their relationship. She enjoys being at home and keeping up with their three boys. Three years ago she started a catering service with a friend that has done very well. She and Tom can talk about the weekly plans and what needs to be done in order to get the boys to school and to soccer games and practices. Things seem to be going well between them.

But something's been missing. Lately Julia's been feeling depressed. She can get things done around the house, and she goes to work and back, but she's had little energy for anything else. She didn't know what was wrong until he took time to take a good look inside.

What she discovered when she assessed the level in her tank was that there had been an increase in tension for her at work. She enjoys her catering work and makes a decent amount of money, but lately there's been a history of ongoing tension with her partner. What she discovered when she looked at her tank was that the level of tension between them had been greater lately. She'd given her partner some of her choices, lowering the level in her tank. She needed to take some steps to change things in that relationship. She'd let her partner have her way with too many recent decisions about their business. Julia needed to speak up and take back her power.

In addition, there were some dissatisfactions with her marriage that needed to be addressed. Her communication with her husband had become so routine that it wasn't fulfilling to her. She wanted more of an exchange of energy in her conversations with her husband. She wanted the deeper intimacy which could result from deeper sharing, adding energy to her tank. Julia also realized that she'd become bored with her sexual relationship with her husband. Sex between them had become mundane. Kids-in-the-bed,-lights-out,-quickie-in-the-missionary-position sex wasn't satisfying. She wanted more of a sense of adventure in the bedroom. Talking, touching, trying new positions—she wanted some changes that would make sex more exciting.

When Julia identified what she wanted, she was able to talk to her husband about it. To her delight, she found that he, too, was open to some experimentation in their sex life. She wanted more time to talk before they touched. They added back rubs and candles to their routine. A occasional bath together and experimentation with new positions led to a revitalized sexual relationship!

Out of Touch—Hindered Choices

Being out of touch with your emotions results in an invalidation of your self. Like Julia, you must learn to stop and listen to yourself. If you don't, the process of seeing available alternatives and making choices will be hindered. Some ways that being out of touch with feelings affects your choices are:

- **Extreme approval seeking.** The part of you that wants acceptance reacts in ways that are designed to secure the approval of the people around you. You ignore or don't act on your feelings, thus emptying your tank.
- **Fear of criticism.** If you're unsure of what you need and want, you'll live in fear of other people's responses. The result is a focus on others which takes away your power to choose.
- **Neglecting yourself while caring for others.** If you haven't assessed the emotional level in your tank, you'll find yourself giving your reserve to others and leaving little for yourself.
- **Perfectionism.** In order to establish more control in your life, you may have turned to perfectionism. This desire to be flawless sets up a tendency to deny parts of yourself or your behavior that seem less than perfect. You'll also struggle with how to handle the conflict between the part of you that seeks perfection and the part of you that knows it's impossible to be perfect!

Getting Back in Touch

There are several ways to restore your access to your emotions. Try any of these as a way to begin the journey back to a connection with yourself. If you want to get the full benefit from these suggestions, you'll need to put your full energy into each one.

I make these suggestions with a sense of fear. These aren't to be taken lightly. They're tools which you can use to accomplish a difficult task. Use them carefully, thoughtfully, and skillfully.

Let me say again that this isn't easy work. There's no recipe you can follow that will plug you back into feelings. This will be difficult, emotional work. For example, you can't attempt breathing for 10 minutes while sitting in front of the television and expect much of a payoff.

Each of these avenues into your emotions is powerful and effective, although one may work better for you than another. Initially, I would suggest you focus on doing one of them for an entire week before going to another one. The more energy you put into this work, the more you'll receive in return.

- **Breathe.** Feel the sensation of the air going into and out of you. Focus on the action of breathing itself. As the air comes into your body, travel down inside yourself with it and investigate what's within you. As you do so, you'll reconnect with your humanness, your passion in life. Rocks and trees don't have lungs, but you do! Allow yourself to feel the power of that life-giving force!

- **Go for a walk.** Walking reinforces a sense of being grounded. Allow your body to communicate to you how you're feeling. If you can, walk in a park or the woods. Being in nature helps you reconnect with your own body. Notice any areas of tension. Feel the sense of progress as you move from one place to another, one step at a time.
- **Write letters you don't intend to mail.** Write to yourself or to any other person, dead or alive, near or far away. Express how you feel. Talk about what hurt or made you uncomfortable. Writing is a catharsis, emptying out the toxins that grow when you hold emotions inside that need to be acted upon. Read your letter out loud and respond to it emotionally.
- **Sit quietly.** Turn off all distractions, including radio and television. Breathe deeply and slowly. Allow yourself to feel. What feelings do you become aware of when you give yourself the opportunity to listen?
- **Have a conversation with someone you trust.** Connecting with a friend, family member or your mate can help you affirm how you're feeling. There's a sense of normalcy that happens when you say, "This is how I'm feeling" and another person says, "I understand!" or "Me too!"
- **Keep an emotional journal.** As you focus on your writing, you'll become more aware of your feelings. You'll have to be honest with how you feel when you write it down. You can't say, "I really didn't feel that way" because you've been honest with yourself. Use the list in this chapter to help you identify a wide range of feelings.
- **Spend an entire day in silence.** Verbiage is one way you may have shielded yourself from your feelings. Being silent can put you back in touch. Become more aware of when you may be talking to protect yourself from how you feel.
- **Focus on your sense of touch.** Feel the wind in your hair. Taste your food as you eat. Allow yourself to enjoy the sensation of putting lotion on your hands. Feel the carpet under your feet as you walk barefoot in the house. Plugging into physical sensation can open the door to greater emotional awareness.
- **Listen to music or watch a movie which touches an emotional chord in you.** Let the music open a door to the emotion

If You Can't Say No You Can't Really Say Yes

within you. Watch a movie with an emotional theme. Let the images open up feeling inside of you.

The most important aspect of getting back in touch with your feelings is permission: giving yourself permission to feel the way you feel and when it's appropriate, to share the way you feel. Your ***personal power to choose*** will be enhanced as you reestablish a connection with your emotions. There's no short cut around it!

POWER TO CHOOSE: How are you feeling?

Emotionally

_____

_____

_____

Physically

_____

_____

_____

Spiritually

_____

_____

_____

Relationally

_____

_____

_____

Look back to page 76 if you need some help with feeling words.

7

COOLING THE VOLCANO
Expressing Anger in a Healthy Manner

THERE IS A PLETHORA of emotions. One list I've seen lists 250 emotion words. But of all emotions, the one men and women often have the greatest difficulty with is anger. As tough as it is to deal with anger effectively, there is a payoff. Learning to handle anger appropriately can do more to help you regain your power to choose than any other single factor.

Anger has gotten a lot of bad press. The truth is, anger as an emotion isn't bad, wrong, or undesirable. Anger is a natural, beneficial, very human feeling. What you need to learn is how to feel your anger and respond to it in a way that's beneficial.

Remember that emotions, especially strong ones like anger, can't be argued with. If you're angry, telling yourself you shouldn't be will have little positive effect. Your feelings are *yours*. You can't deny them without negative consequences.

Learning from Your Anger

Consider the example of one couple whose relationship was being damaged by destructive anger. When Phil and Lana came to my office, the first thing that really struck me was that this relatively calm and otherwise easy going man had become so angry and vengeful. They both expressed surprise at the way Phil's anger had become so intense. Lana felt hurt and amazed at the way her husband had recently begun to explode at her in anger.

Phil said he was angry because Lana was always demanding something of him. It seemed to him that she was constantly bothering him, requesting his help with some problem she had. He said he was tired of bailing her out and wished she "would just leave me alone!" Even though they'd been reasonably happy for several years, Phil had grown so tired of this style of marriage and was so pessimistic that things would ever change, he'd lately begun talking about divorce. It was obvious to me as he talked that his tank was nearing empty.

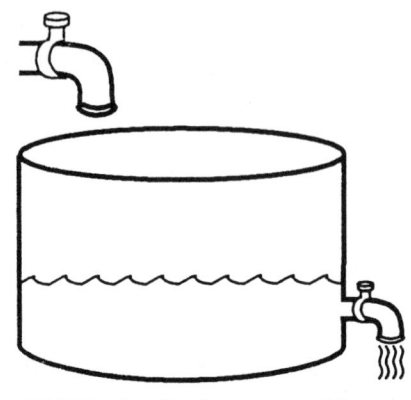

Tank depleted by constant problems.

Phil had talked to some friends about his problems with Lana, but they ignored his anger and emphasized that he would just have to work it out. He was told that all couples have problems and that he'd just have to be tough. Some of his church friends only responded to his comment that he "sometimes wanted just to get out" of the marriage, by saying, "You know God says that you can't get divorced!" But no one could tell Phil how to handle his anger.

Counseling began with my seeing him individually a few times. We explored his anger and disappointment. The counseling room was a safe place for him to acknowledge and investigate his anger. Here he didn't have to fear being criticized or put down for how he felt. As we explored his anger, we found some answers.

The relationship between Phil and Lana got off to a fast start while the two of them were still in high school. Their involvement had deepened quickly because Lana couldn't get along with her mother. Lana's perspective was that any time she differed with what her mother thought she should think or how she should behave, her mother criticized her. They would have long, loud, emotional arguments. After they started dating, Lana would call Phil after these arguments with her mother and tell him all the hurtful details of the most recent row. During the time they dated, Phil spent hour upon hour attempting to console her over the telephone. Sometimes he would come pick her up and take her out in order to cheer her up. A few times he even tried to be a peacemaker between his wife-to-be and her mother.

This style of relating was a powerful force in bringing Phil and Lana together. This aspect of their relationship dance brought them into close contact and kept them emotionally involved. After they married, this pattern continued with Lana experiencing problems with her mom and Phil's making valiant efforts to help improve things. Phil remained the problem-solver and Lana faithfully provided him with problems to solve. After four years, he'd grown tired of this arrangement, but couldn't see any way to alter it. His emotional response was an intense anger which signaled to him that he couldn't continue this way.

Intense anger signals the need for boundary changes.

Things began to change when Phil stopped to listen to his anger instead of denying it or saying, "I shouldn't feel like this!" When he could listen, he recognized that his anger was present for a reason. This emotion was a signal to him that he felt taken advantage of in his marriage. When he stopped to listen to his anger, he began to see options which could change his marriage and allow the two of them to live in a more satisfying way.

Phil's first move was to focus more on himself and what he needed. He stepped out of the "Henry Kissinger" role he'd adopted by removing himself from the ongoing problems between Lana and her mother. In conjoint sessions with his wife, we focused on ways in which she could handle her own problems with her mom. Phil set some clear boundaries which worked to change his role to that of a supportive listener rather than an overly involved fixer.

The changes came slowly and were hard to stick to. Old patterns die hard. They learned a new dance over a period of several months which allowed both of them to have a marriage in which they didn't need a problem to keep them close.

Six years later I checked in with them. They're still happily married. Each has learned the importance of setting limits with significant people in their lives. The changes in their marital relationship had generalized into other areas. They'd set firm limits with co-workers, employers and friends. They're expecting their third child and are looking forward to the experience.

Here's the lesson for regaining choices: Only when Phil was able to tune in and listen to his anger was he able to benefit from this powerful and valuable emotion. When he could allow himself to experience his feelings, he began to take the steps necessary to change his situation.

Rules Against Expressing Anger

It's not uncommon to develop some strong rules against expressing anger. These rules can come from your parents, your church or your sense of what society expects. Some of these rules or restraints are:
- Anger is a waste of emotional energy.
- Don't let them know they got to you!
- God would *not* approve!
- You might get out of control.
- Only the people in charge can get angry.
- If I get angry, I'll have to hurt something or someone.

So long as you're following any of these rules, feeling, expressing and handling anger will be impossible. Only when you choose to accept your anger as being as much a part of life as your joy, sadness or satisfaction can you live a healthy and whole life. Only when you embrace your anger can your sense of self and your ***personal power to choose*** be maximized.

Accepting and expressing your anger isn't the same as blaming everyone else in your world for your problems and/or taking your anger out on others by yelling, threatening or hitting. Any form of angry touch is abusive and can damage the reserve tank as well as deplete it's reserve. No one should have to tip-toe around you just so they won't "make" you angry. No one can make you angry without your help. You have to take responsibility for your anger and any way that you choose to express it.

Learning About Anger in Your Family

In many families, the only emotion which was expressed with any consistency was anger. And the only people in the family who could be angry were the big people. The children weren't supposed to be angry, but with such a compelling parental role model, it was difficult not to be.

Cooling the Volcano

Actually, you could have been angry and probably were. It was just unacceptable for you to express it to your parents. Being angry, yet having to stuff or deny this powerful emotion, is a very frustrating way to live. The only answer for some of you was to numb out. You don't feel anything. Sometimes you've used drugs, alcohol, food or work to help you stay numb. Others of you let your anger come out sideways by expressing anger at anyone else besides the true object of your anger. You might be angry at your boss, but take it out on your spouse or children. Men often learn to vent their considerable store of anger by engaging in manly pursuits: contact sports, collecting and shooting guns, killing of animals. Women often express their anger in more passive/aggressive ways, looking "nice" the entire time. It's a lot easier in the short-term to be "nice," to smile and do for others and let yourself be taken advantage of, than to risk expressing the anger that has built up inside of you. In the long run, being taken advantage of is very depleting to the level in your tank.

There was a lot of anger expressed in Teresa's family as she was growing up, but only by one member of her family: her dad. Her father was the only one with permission to exhibit his anger. His anger was frightening to Teresa. When her dad was mad, she always responded in two ways. First, she would get anxious, concerned that some unnamed and unpredictable bad something would happen. "What's he going to do this time?" she wondered. Her anxiety led to a huge knot in her stomach. Second, she would scurry around to see what she could do to please her father so he wouldn't have any additional reasons to become more angry. One of Teresa's goals as she worked to become more healthy was to learn how to deal with anger—her own and the anger of others—in more effective ways.

For Teresa, being around angry people often has resulted in that familiar knot in her gut, even if they aren't angry at her. She remembered going to a fast food restaurant one morning for breakfast and hearing the shift manager yelling at his employees behind the counter. Teresa's stomach began to tighten up in sympathy for those who were targets of the manager's angry-sounding demands.

After she'd listened to this angry exchange for a minute or more, she stopped eating and looked around the dining room. No one else seemed to be hearing or reacting to the words that were so overwhelming to her. Even though she'd intended to stay at her table for awhile as she finished a project for work, she chose to leave so she could find a quieter, less stressful place. Another person might have chosen to have a word with the manager, but she chose to leave.

Using Anger to Protect Yourself

Kyle had an experience recently which indicated how far he'd come in allowing himself to listen to and respond to his anger. It also showed him that he still had much to learn about feeling and expressing anger effectively.

Last night Kyle was extremely angry at his friend, Chris. They engaged in a very loud and confrontational argument with each other. It happened quickly. In a flash it started and within minutes it was over. Kyle cursed Chris. They stared at each other in disbelief as the argument continued. Kyle felt he'd been challenged to take care of himself and he responded forcefully.

Chris and Kyle play tennis on Monday nights. They talk before they play, during warm-ups, and as they exchange sides of the net. It's more than a tennis game and something they both look forward to each week.

Kyle was the one who erupted last night. As the game began, Chris mentioned to him that he was angry. Their time together lately had been clouded by Chris' struggles in dealing with a dating relationship he was in. The woman he was involved with was the focus of many of their conversations. His anger at her had affected a number of their Monday night games as he would attempt to work off his frustrations by hitting the ball after the point was over, yelling to release his frustration, "talking trash" to Kyle to regain a sense of his personal power, and occasionally throwing his racket. The knot in Kyle's gut would sometimes grow in response to Chris' anger. Kyle would ask him if he was angry at him and he always said, "No." Kyle's tack before last night had been to attempt to remain detached from Chris' anger, hoping he would soon learn to express it in a different way. He tried to stay detached from Chris' anger. Some weeks he was better at it than others.

The Monday before last night they'd been unable to play. Chris had called at the last minute to cancel because he said he had some things he wanted to discuss with his girlfriend. Kyle told him that he was disappointed that they couldn't play. Later that week they were able to get together and Kyle expressed to Chris his disappointment that he'd canceled their game. He was angry that Chris' relationship with his girlfriend so often negatively affected their friendship and their tennis matches. They had a sober and productive conversation that Kyle thought ended with a commitment that Chris' relationship with the woman in his life wouldn't so directly affect their time together.

When Chris arrived for the night's match, he mentioned that he was angry. Kyle assumed he meant at his girlfriend, but he didn't talk to Chris about it. He said later that he was no doubt on edge even as they started since Chris made it a point to mention his anger.

They were both rusty after not playing for a couple of weeks. As Chris looked for the intensity of his game, he became more aggressive. He made a couple of comments, like, "We really have our own styles of play, don't we?" which was said in a sarcastic tone. Kyle took these as more than comments. They sounded like judgments. They were followed by more of what he called "trash talk."

Finally, Kyle had all he wanted. He spoke up, expressing the anger he'd held inside over the past few weeks. He didn't think about it. He didn't edit what came out. He just set a boundary with his anger.

"Don't mess with me tonight, Chris!" he declared. Only he didn't say "mess." He said the F word. He'd never cursed at him in the two years they'd known each other.

"What did you say?" Chris asked incredulously. Kyle was sure Chris thought he'd misunderstood him.

"Don't mess with me tonight. Just play the game. Don't bring your frustrations with your girlfriend in here for me to deal with." Chris' response was curt. He said he was dealing with it and that Kyle should leave it alone.

They finished that game. As Kyle went to the net to bounce Chris the tennis balls so he could serve, more words were exchanged.

"Don't be talking that trash at me tonight! I'm tired of it and I don't have to hear it," Kyle said.

"You're the only one talking trash, Kyle. Not me!" he exclaimed. "I was just playing my game." They were standing face to face on opposite sides of the net.

They two of them made enough noise that the men on the next court became concerned. While neither Kyle nor Chris thought it was any of their business, they threatened to go get someone to quiet them down or escort them out.

"Let's just play the game!" Kyle remembered saying that several times. After that game they exchanged sides. As Kyle walked toward Chris, he apologized for the language he'd chosen to express himself. But he felt no need to apologize for speaking up. They exchanged a hug and grins and went on with the match, which, by the way, Chris won.

Afterwards, they walked and talked about what had happened. Chris had his own perspective, but his didn't negate Kyle's. They both shared some additional information which helped them understand what had happened.

Things weren't rosy afterwards. In fact, it took several months of talking before they were able play tennis without difficult reflections on that night they'd argued.

For Kyle, that argument felt powerful and cleansing. It was also very imperfect. He'd waited much too long to say what he needed to say. By the time he spoke up, he was too emotionally charged to communicate effectively. He knew that he still had a long way to go in learning to deal with his anger in a healthy way. He needed more practice.

While neither one of them said things in the best way, Kyle and Chris expressed some things that they needed to say in order to take care of themselves. That's really the purpose of healthy anger. And they were able to walk away from it still friends.

Handling Your Anger

Feeling and expressing your anger is messy work. In fact, you could say that expressing your anger is like giving an elephant an enema. Sometimes it's absolutely essential to do so, but it's a very big job and it's hard to go through the process without getting some manure on yourself!

There are positive ways to deal with your anger. The goal is to handle rather than be handled by your anger. Try these suggestions as you attempt to restore your personal power with respect to anger:

- **Face your anger**. Deal with it. Don't deny it. Only when you truly grapple with your anger instead of reacting to it can any resolution come. You may not want to admit you're angry. Honestly look at yourself.

    You have to risk being vulnerable in order to express your anger in a constructive way. Yelling keeps people at a distance. To say, "I'm furious with you!" in an emotional, yet controlled tone takes courage. It's not easy to do.

- **Express your anger** to the person or persons with whom you're angry. Do it as soon as you're ready. The longer you wait, the more difficult it often becomes. Ask yourself, "Who am I angry at? What am I angry about?" Avoid expressing your anger to people you aren't angry at. That's like kicking the dog because you're angry at your spouse.

Andrea knew that she was often too angry because of relatively minor inconveniences and frustrations in her life. Getting in the slowest line at the bank or supermarket was infuriating for her. When she looked inside with a careful and discriminating eye, she found that she'd been stockpiling unexpressed anger for a long time. This accumulated anger was like a big bucket of energy that she tapped into when she was angry about other, minor irritations in her life. Andrea became convinced that if she was to be more appropriate with her anger in the present, she needed to get current and stay current with her anger. She worked at emptying the big bucket of old anger so that it wasn't such a hindrance to her expressing current anger.

- **Cultivate your freedom to express the wide range of human emotions**. You may be frustrated, but that isn't the same as being angry. Being afraid may not feel powerful, but reacting to feelings of fear by being angry won't resolve the fear. Doing so keeps you stuck and empties your tank.

  Most of the time, there's something infinitely more exciting and/or interesting underneath the anger that you feel. Anger is often a defense for feelings and issues that will eventually need to be the true focus of your attention. Only when you're ready to strip away the anger you've used as a protective shield can any real progress be made at resolving your situation.

- As a short-term aid, it may be beneficial to **find a positive outlet for your anger**. Driving 95 MPH is *not* a healthy way to express anger. A long walk, chopping wood, twisting a towel, beating on a pillow, playing racquetball or some other form of physical exertion while visualizing yourself being connected with your angry feelings can be healthy expressions. When your stress level is lower, take steps to deal with the issues contributing to your anger.

- **Write out your anger**. Create your own *Mad Magazine*, a notebook you can use to empty out the anger inside. Writing will also help you focus your attention on the problem, your feelings and potential solutions.

- **When you're ready to express your anger, do it as directly as possible**. Accept responsibility for your emotions. Begin by expressing your anger rather than by sermonizing or accusing.

"I am angry because you forgot to meet me after work!" will be much easier to hear than, "You're such a forgetful dope!"
- **Resist the notion that you have to do anger perfectly.** If you attempt to be perfect, you'll either shy away from anger until you think you can do it right or you'll beat yourself up after expressing anger if you believe it came out wrong. Either extreme will hamper your efforts.

Anger isn't an end in itself. It's a way for you to assess when and where you need to set a boundary in order to protect yourself or to help you meet a need. Use this emotion to help direct your life and take care of yourself. In this way you can reclaim parts of yourself which have been lost to others.

POWER TO CHOOSE: One thing you could do to help yourself deal with your anger more appropriately would be:

_____

_____

_____

The most difficult challenge you face in responding to your anger is:

_____

_____

_____

8

CAREFULLY FOLLOWING POOR MAPS
How the Scripts You Follow Can Affect Your Choices

SEVERAL YEARS AGO my family moved to Nashville, Tennessee. Since the city was new to us and since we were unfamiliar with it, we purchased a street map that would assist us in getting around town. What I didn't know at the time was that the map we'd acquired didn't reflect changes which had been made in several streets in one area of the city. A major construction project involving several miles of new interstate had cut through scores of streets. Streets that were shown on the map as through streets no longer were!

I can calmly describe these changes now, but at the time I felt quite angry and frustrated. I knew where I wanted to go, but I couldn't get there. The map indicated that what I was attempting to do would work, when in fact it wouldn't. Even when I carefully followed the map, it would only lead me to dead ends. I would back up and try again, only to be led to another frustrating conclusion. No matter how carefully I read and followed the map, my trips into that part of town affected by the construction usually turned out poorly.

A map is helpful only to the degree that it's accurate. A map is just a representation of a territory. It's not the same as the territory; it's a depiction. If a map is inaccurate, it will provoke frustration more often than it will provide help.

Living Life With Your Map

In your journey through life, you'll acquire a map. This map is your view of reality. Note that your map isn't reality; it's your view of reality. There's a big difference.

In the years prior to the time of Columbus, people viewed the world as flat. It was assumed that the earth had edges and that you could fall off those edges. When Columbus sailed off to find the new world, many who saw him leave, and perhaps members of his own crew, thought he'd sail off the edge and never return.

The point is that believing that the world was flat didn't make it flat. This belief did cause the people who held it to behave as if the world were flat. Their map of the world, inaccurate though it was, was the guide by which they lived. The people who lived in Columbus' time considered the flatness of the earth to be true. When he returned from his voyage to the new world and told tales of his adventure, they had a choice to make. If they believed that Columbus had actually sailed around the world, their map needed to be challenged. A flat earth map wouldn't work any longer.

You're a participant in creating the kind of world you live in. You're actively involved in constructing your own world view. Your experiences and your interpretation of and reactions to those experiences work together to make you the person that you are. To illustrate the principle, let me relate a fascinating story, the story of the creation of a neurotic horse.

Following an Outdated Map

Researchers constructed a stall with a metal floor through which an electrical charge could be sent. In the stall, they placed a horse. When the researchers sent a charge of electricity through the floor, the horse was bothered by an uncomfortable, although of course not harmful, shock. The horse soon discovered that if he lifted one hoof, the shock would cease. The horse showed that he could adapt to his surroundings. The researchers then added step two of their experiment. They would sound a bell before sending the shock. The horse was able to tie the two events together. He found that he could avoid the shock altogether if he lifted his leg when he heard the bell. The horse once again showed his ability to change his behavior in response to his environment.

After the horse had applied this "map" to his situation, the researchers went on to step three. They continued to sound the bell, but ceased sending the electrical charge. The horse continued to lift his leg when he heard the bell and of course wasn't shocked since there was no longer any current to shock him. The horse never verified the continued need for lifting his hoof, apparently sure of his assumption that lifting his hoof was sparing him the shock he wanted to avoid.

Can you see the picture here? The horse was carefully following an outdated map. His way of adapting to his former environment was healthy and resourceful. But continuing to follow his old map when his world had changed created unnecessary effort and concern for him. He exhibited behavior that in a human would be described as "neurotic."

Many of you who have only two legs have spent years following an outdated or ineffective map. For instance, if you grew up in an alcoholic family, you may have learned not to trust other people nor to express your emotions. If you spoke up to a father who had been drinking, you might have been abused verbally or physically. Keeping your opinions and feelings to yourself may have been effective and perhaps life-saving adaptations in that home setting. However, to continue to follow that map when you're in a relationship with a friend or a spouse who loves you and wouldn't seek to wound you is very much like that neurotic horse who followed the old rules when the situation had changed.

Many of you have spent years following a map which simply read, "Be Nice!" You thought that if you did enough for others, they would love you and accept you. You hoped that if you allowed others to have their way, they would thank you for your willingness to give. You firmly believed that doing enough of the right things would be the way to prove your worth and to receive the affirmation you had searched for since childhood. You thought you had to give up yourself in order to maintain your relationships. In short, you gave up your power and your choices for the sake of your relationships.

This map won't work. It'll be as frustrating as that map of Nashville which I acquired. Doing for others doesn't make them love you, nor will it cause you to love yourself. Always giving in to others will leave you feeling used, bitter and resentful, especially when your niceness isn't reciprocated by the people around you. And being nice will never result in your feeling more loved since *doing* never contributes to feeling loved.

To live by this sort of guide is to carefully follow a poor map. If the quality of your life is to improve, you must question the authenticity of your map. You must question the underlying premises. The more the map reflects the actual territory, the better you'll feel about yourself and your life. You'll also experience a greater level of success.

When Your Map Doesn't Work

Harriet believed that if she allowed her husband to have his way in their relationship, he would love and respect her more. Whatever he wanted she worked to provide because she thought that sooner or later he would see how hard she was trying and would love her more for it. Whatever he wanted to buy, whenever he wanted to go out to dinner, whomever he wanted to have over, whatever he wanted when they made love, she was agreeable. Her map said that if she did enough of these things, her spouse would reciprocate. When he didn't, she felt used, but she attempted to cover those feelings. She didn't want him to know how disappointed she was becoming. Harriet attempted to cover her resentment, but of course it would come through in covert ways. The level in her reserve tank stayed at a chronically low level.

Giving for years without receiving leads to a low level.

The final indication to her that this map of the world wasn't going to get her to the destination she desired was that her husband had an affair with her best friend. When she first found out, Harriet was only angry with herself. She told herself that if she'd been a better wife, if she'd been more loving, if she'd been a more exciting lover, then he wouldn't have had the affair. But something about that perspective didn't feel right. She knew she'd done all she could to please him and she still didn't get what she wanted. Slowly she questioned her map. She allowed herself to feel just how angry she was with her friend. Later she became conscious of the great amount of anger she felt toward her husband.

Harriet began to question the contents of her entire map. She realized that she hadn't behaved in a way that commanded respect. In fact, her husband didn't have to give her a second thought. She initiated the long process of changing her attitude and behavior. She became more aware of how she felt. She began to ask for more from her husband. If he didn't want to do something she suggested, like going to a movie, she considered going to do it by herself. When she told a friend that she'd gone out to eat by herself after her husband reneged on his promise to take her out, she knew that her map had really changed. This greater sense of detachment gave her a sense of independence which freed her from the tyranny of attempting to please her spouse all the time.

How Your Map Affects You

Have you ever wondered why one person is afraid of water while another person takes to water like a fish? Why is it that one of your friends seems to be a natural at public speaking while another friend who grew up in the same neighborhood can't even deliver a speech to himself in the mirror? Have you noticed that two people from similar ethnic backgrounds can have widely differing views of people from another cultural heritage?

Your map is your guide in all areas of your life. These diagrams reflect your view of God, organized religion, family, career choices, friendship, recreation, and the use of mood altering substances. Your map will dictate whether you take chances or play it safe. It's an interpretive guide that you use constantly to filter and organize the events of your life.

Consider how persons with differing maps could have varied responses to the following circumstances:

- A family of a different culture or background moves in next door.
- One of your children is failing English in school.
- You go to the beach on spring break and it rains all week.
- Your boss finds the quality of your work unacceptable and chastises you in angry tones in front of your co-workers.
- Your spouse seems to prefer eating in front of the television every evening, while you would like to eat at the table and talk.
- You go to a movie and the couple behind you loudly comments on each scene.
- One of the children spills a glass of milk at dinner.
- Tornadoes touch down in your area destroying several homes, but yours isn't harmed.
- Someone you know tells you he doesn't like something you're doing.
- Someone you know tells you he likes something you're doing.
- Someone you don't know tells you he doesn't like something you're doing.

If you hold the view that strangers are to be feared, then your response to meeting someone you don't know on the street in a strange city would be much different than that of a person who perceived strangers simply as "people I just don't yet know." If you believe that when people suffer, it's always because God is punishing them for their sins, you'll filter your life experiences in a much different way than will a person who believes that God is a being of love and that sometimes bad things happen to people. Your attitude directly affects what fills and empties your tank.

The story is told of a revered man in a small village in China. His horse escaped one night and his neighbors took it upon themselves to offer their consolation. They lamented his unfortunate loss saying, "It's so terrible that you've lost your horse!" His only response was, "How do you know?" The next day his stallion returned leading a herd of twenty fine, wild horses. His neighbors congratulated him on his gain. "You are indeed a fortunate man!" they proclaimed. His only response was, "How do you know?" The next day his teenage son was thrown from one of the horses as he attempted to tame it. When he fell, he broke his leg. Again the neighbors expressed their condolences at this turn of fate. "This is a terrible thing that has happened!" they exclaimed. Again the old man's response was simply, "How do you know?" The next day the military came through town conscripting every able-bodied young man. Because his son had a broken leg, he wasn't forced to go into battle.

Is what has happened to you "fortunate" or "terrible," or is it just part of the unfolding story of your life? In this story, the neighbors' view differed from that of the old man even though they were all observing the same events. In the same way, your perception of the events which happen to you will be determined by your map.

An Inside Look

Take a look at your map. What are some of the rules and messages you're using as a guide? Do you find these beneficial? Are there some that you don't find helpful? Is your tank being filled or emptied by the restraints of your map?

Many of the rules you follow were learned at home. Some were learned through your religious ties. Others were developed in interaction with others in your world. Stop and do a self-assessment of your map.

Carefully Following Poor Maps

1. Some rules I have learned that I find helpful are:

_____
_____

2. Some rules I have learned that I struggle with are:

_____
_____

3. Some rules I learned that I have already rejected are:

_____
_____

4. Rules I would like to own, but haven't been able to adopt so far are:

_____
_____

In my work with clients, I have heard them describe rules which fall into all of these categories. For instance, "Don't feel the way you feel!" is a common religious and parental rule, a rule which doesn't lead to productive living. It's often one that men and women decide to change.

There's no reason to reject all the rules you've been taught. Many of them are good and healthy. Rules you might choose to keep could include, "Treat other people with respect" and "Children are a gift, not a possession."

Your map for parenting may have to be extensively modified for you to be as effective a parent as you want to be. Some of the old rules you may have to challenge would be:

- Spank first. Get names and ask questions later.
- When a parent feels out of control, exerting more control will bring things back under control.
- Yelling is an effective means of communicating important, parental wisdom.
- It's more important for a father to make extra money than it is for him to be at home with the children when they are young.
- If you appear big enough, your children will see themselves as small and will respond as children should: hesitantly, always seeking to do what parents want.
- Never let your children see that you're hurt.
- If all else fails, guilt your children into doing what you see is best. After all, it's "for their own good!"

Changing Your Map

Revamping your map requires time, dedication to the task and lots of effort. Changes don't come easily. You'll have to work hard to alter your guide. Circumstances change over time and your map will need to be updated in order to accommodate the new information. Constant assessment is necessary to help you keep up with the pieces of your present reality.

Your map has four major components. Your views and your rules will fall somewhere in these four areas. The parts of your map can be summarized in this way:

1. How you feel about yourself, your level of self-esteem. When you feel good about yourself, you'll act, feel and think differently than you do when you don't like yourself. The only way to improve your relationships with others is to focus on improving the quality of your relationship with yourself. The work you've been doing to reclaim your choices will lead to an increase in your level of self-esteem.

2. Style of communicating. Your map reflects the way you were taught to communicate. Virginia Satir suggests several basic categories: the distracter, the blamer, the placater, the computer and the leveler. Distracters create a commotion hoping no one will actually notice them. Blamers point their finger at others so they don't have to face their own imperfections. Placators seek to do whatever others want in an effort to please them and gain approval. Computers are like robots, totally out of touch with their emotions. Levelers are the genuine communicators, those who can directly express themselves. Obviously, this last group are those who are best equipped to live a life filled with healthy choices.

3. Rules are rules! In some families, accepting the rules and keeping the rules sovereignly reigns. Rules were more important than relationships. In other families, rules are intended to serve the needs of the people in the family. If it becomes apparent that a particular rule no longer has a positive function, steps are taken to change it.

4. Connection with the outside world. Can the people "out there" be trusted? How close can you allow yourself to get to those outside your family?

Your map can be altered as you focus on changes in these areas.

Two Stories of Change

Marvin was the oldest of four children and the only son. His father was gone from home most of the time to one of his two jobs. He spent most of his family time with his sisters and his mother. Without meaning to do so, Marvin's mother came to rely heavily on him for support. Even as a student in grade school, he would have adult conversations with his mom about how she felt and her frustration with the fact that his dad was gone so much.

Marvin came to feel responsible for making life better for his mom. He would write her notes, bring her flowers, and give her hugs and kisses. When she looked sad, he would attempt to cheer her up. His extra duties as a surrogate spouse cut into his time to be a kid. He received more attention when he took care of his mother than when he took care of himself. He learned well the lesson of tending to the needs of the woman in his life before meeting any needs of his own.

When he married, he continued to follow this map which called for him to please his wife before himself. His only sense of personal well-being came from doing what he thought his wife would like. He couldn't communicate what he wanted and needed because that would be a violation of the rule. It would also be selfish. He spent no time away from home without his wife except for his time at work. Marvin was very active with the children, prepared dinner many times each week, cleaned house regularly and mowed the grass to perfection each weekend between April and October. In many ways he looked like the ideal husband.

Inside things weren't going so well with Marvin. He felt empty and neglected. His tank became more and more depleted. While he could talk to his wife and listen to her problems, he didn't share his needs and issues. He finally reached a point where he a choice to make: either change the map to allow himself to be genuine and an equal partner with his spouse *or* slowly cease to exist. He chose the former.

Carmen was another person who was following an outdated map. She learned a difficult and important rule when she was still a child: Men don't stay! They will get unhappy with you, but be unable to tell you so. There will come a point when they've had all they can take, and one day they'll be gone. She learned this lesson when as a teenager of thirteen, her dad left her mom and cut off all contact with the family. She'd received no prior warning; suddenly, her dad was just gone.

In the years after he left, dad spent little time with her. He and his new wife very quickly had a child, and his time and attention shifted to his new family. An occasional day here and there and a perfunctory visit at Christmas were all she could expect. In effect, when her dad moved out of the house, he moved out of her life. To make things worse for her, the next year her grandfather, with whom she'd felt a close and special bond, died unexpectedly of a heart attack.

When she started dating, this "Men don't stay!" message played an influential role. She was jealous of anyone else the young man she was dating even looked at, much less talked to. When he was late to pick her up, she was convinced that he'd left her for someone else.

Carmen married soon after graduation from college, hoping she'd found a man who wouldn't leave her, but not being fully convinced that she had. She followed the old map, but attempted to keep her insecurities from her husband. She coped by keeping an emotional, physical and sexual distance between them. Occasionally her husband would comment that he sensed an aloofness about her and a vague sense that she didn't trust him. Of course she would deny it all, redoubling her efforts to look better so he wouldn't catch on. She would secretly vow that she would do a better job at masking her inability to get close. But no one is that good. You can't just pretend your way through life, not if you want to live life to the fullest.

Eventually Carmen realized that her map wasn't getting her what she wanted. This is always the first step toward change. She began to question the components of her map, especially her rules about not being able to rely on men. "Who says?" became her favorite phrase. If she heard one of the old rules being shouted out in her head, she would question it by asking, "Who says?" "He's late. He's probably with someone else!" she might hear her untrusting side say. "Who says?" she learned to answer. She attempted to respond to her husband based on what was happening between them now instead of being controlled by old rules that she learned in dealing with her father's abandoning her and her grandfather's death.

She spent lots of energy focusing on her own unmet needs for love and acceptance. She hadn't felt loved by her father. Her mother was so busy after the divorce just making a living and holding the family together that she didn't always have time for Carmen. She had a love wound, a deep, large void inside where love was supposed to be, but wasn't. She needed to experience unconditional love, love that a person receives just because he or she exists. She made fewer implied demands that her husband should love her like she wanted to be loved.

She realized that no one else could heal her wound; she was the only person who could do it.

In the process of this challenging work, Carmen developed a new way of looking at herself and her world. In effect, she updated her map. She cultivated her level of self-acceptance. She grew to love herself more. In the process, she was able to make the choice to allow herself greater closeness to her husband. Her new map allowed her the intimacy with him that the old map had denied.

Suggestions for Challenging Your Map

Your map is your creation. With effort and persistence, you can change it. Altering your map can allow you new choices which are more productive, more up-to-date and appropriate to the present situation.

Try the following suggestions as you update your map:

1. Recognize that change is possible. You aren't the powerless result of your history. You can choose to change. Realize your personal power!

2. Accept the way you think and feel. Begin right where you are, even if it isn't where you want to be. Remember, feelings just exist. They can't be argued with.

3. Challenge your belief system. Ask yourself, "Do I hold some beliefs that don't allow for or contribute to my happiness?" Remember that your emotions are the result of the meaning you attach to them. You can hold some interpretations which will deplete your tank. Some interpretations which tend to empty your tank are:

- I must be loved and approved of by every significant person in my life.
- When people behave badly or unfairly, they should be blamed and punished.
- It's awful when things don't go the way I'd like for them to.
- The world should be fair and just.
- It's easier to avoid than to face life's difficulties.

4. Allow for differences in people. No two of us are alike. Avoid attempting to make yourself like someone else or following a map that works for someone else but which may not work for you.

5. Get more information. Read books. Watch videos. Attend lectures. Join a support group. Learn all you can.

The next two chapters will discuss the maps that women and men in our culture often come to accept. Following these poor maps often

If You Can't Say No You Can't Really Say Yes

lead to disappointment and frustration. Challenging these roles can lead to a life of greater satisfaction.

POWER TO CHOOSE: Stop and take a careful look at your map.

1. Who or what has been the most influential force in constructing your map?

_____

_____

_____

2. Are you satisfied with the map you're following?

_____

_____

_____

3. What one step could you take today to update your map?

_____

_____

_____

9

"SUGAR AND SPICE AND EVERYTHING NICE"
Crippling Elements of Women's Roles

THE NURSERY RHYME proclaims that girls are made of "sugar and spice and everything nice." Does that imply that women must always smell nice and be nice? Are women required to be able to get along with everyone else? What if you don't feel nice today? Or sweet? Does that make you any less a woman? Just as men have been sold a bill of goods when it comes to the role they're to play, as you'll see in the next chapter, so women have been asked to be less than and different than themselves in order to meet our culture's definition of femininity.

Let me say at the outset that I feel terribly inadequate to describe fully the experience women have had in living out their roles and dealing with cultural expectations. I don't claim to have all the answers, but I do believe I have a few. In preparation for writing what you'll read in the next few pages, I have called upon my experience in facilitating women's groups for the last six years. I have seen more women than men in my clinical practice during the last fifteen years, so I have listened as hundreds of women have told me their stories. In addition, I interviewed several of my fellow therapists who are female and obtained their feedback on what they felt needed to be said in this chapter, although I alone am responsible for the form that feedback takes.

It's Not Supposed to Be Like This!

Let's begin by considering a case study of one woman and her attempt to find happiness in her marriage. When Katherine married Eddie, she was awash in dreams of happily ever after. She'd created vivid mental pictures of wedded bliss—two children, maybe three, a three-bedroom brick home in the suburbs, nice cars and a serene, stable life. What she got instead was disappointment, criticism and heartache.

She'd been taught that a woman's job was to be nurturing to her children and supportive of her husband. Their needs came before her own. If she cleaned and cooked and carried and cared enough, not only her family, but she herself would be content. This was the model of womanhood she'd been taught. She attempted to follow it to the letter.

She stayed home and had babies. She fed them and cared for them. She kept the house, cleaning and decorating so that it could be something her husband would be proud to come home to. She cooked hearty meals and tasty desserts. "The way to a man's heart is through his stomach." She'd heard that for years.

Katherine dieted and exercised to keep herself fit and appealing. She not only made herself available for Eddie sexually, but looked forward to their intimate times together. She was a willing and enthusiastic partner.

She performed what she thought was her role, but Eddie didn't come through with his part of the arrangement. For instance, he worked, but he didn't always bring his paycheck home. Katherine often had to beg for money even for necessities like food. Money for new clothes for the children was almost impossible to come by.

When Eddie came home at all, he spent most of his time criticizing Katherine and yelling at the children. He was away from home a lot with his friends, usually just hanging out and drinking. Katherine pleaded with him to come home so she and the children could spend time with him, but he seldom listened to her. He said he needed time to relax.

Eddie frequently didn't come home at night, choosing to sleep in the beds of other women instead. To Katherine this was the ultimate slap in the face. She'd tried so hard to please him, and this was what she received in return?

Something had gone very wrong with her picture of family perfection. Katherine knew early in the marriage that this wasn't the way things were supposed to be, but she didn't know what to do. Her plan hadn't worked. Her training hadn't prepared her for such a disastrous outcome. She was beginning to feel empty and tired.

Katherine hadn't been taught how to confront such problems. She certainly didn't believe she could tell anyone about how unhappy she was. For a long time she held on to her dream of a happy family. Using the same model, she just tried harder. Maybe she wasn't doing

"Sugar and Spice and Everything Nice"

her jobs well enough. Surely if she worked at it, she could win his love and approval. A cleaner house, children that were well behaved, better meals, more exercise, some revealing lingerie—she did all she knew to do.

She tried to talk to Eddie about her frustrations, but usually he tuned her out or left the house. She pled with him to make them a family. When they did actually have a conversation, he could turn what she said around and make it all her fault. Eddie didn't listen very often and when he did, he made hollow promises that very seldom came true.

In another desperate attempt to make her marriage work, she tried doing things Eddie's way. She'd get a sitter and stay out late with him, drinking with him and his friends. But she didn't like the way she felt when she drank so much. And she felt awful about being away from her children for this sort of entertainment. This just wasn't the sort of life she was comfortable living.

After several years of frustration, the crying started. Katherine didn't seem to be able to stop it. She tried, but she couldn't make the tears go away. She was depressed and she knew it. The level in her reserve tank was dangerously low.

Low level due to depleting roles.

One day everything changed for Katherine. She'd had enough. One morning the light came on and she realized that she'd long since ceased being a wife, she wasn't being an effective mother and she wasn't a happy person. She'd given herself away until there was barely enough of her left to keep going. She couldn't keep living this way!

From that point forward, things began to change, not with the relationship, but within Katherine herself. She sought the support of her minister. She hadn't told anyone how bad things had been at home—pretending everything was okay was part of the expectation she'd inherited. She poured out her heart to her pastor and found him to be very supportive. She was surprised to discover that he'd seen evidence of the problems for a long time. She wasn't as good at pretending as she'd imagined she was. After Katherine told him, she told two or three friends. Finally, she told her parents.

With some support, Katherine reached deep inside herself and found the strength to divorce. Still, it was an extremely difficult thing for her to do. All the while she grieved the loss of her dream. This wasn't the way her life was supposed to turn out! But no matter how hard she tried, she couldn't make it happen; she couldn't make her family a happy one. Eighteen years later—four children, a bankruptcy and dozens of her husband's affairs later—she was finally forced to admit that this model for womanhood wasn't going to work.

What It Means to be a Woman

My research, my experience and the opinions of my colleagues led to my choosing the case study you've just read. It sums up most of what I've seen and heard when it comes to contemplating women's roles. What I want to illustrate is how the way women are expected to behave often diminishes their power to choose. In the next few pages you'll explore some of the factors involved in the choice-depleting role of women that can be seen in Katherine's story. We'll discuss some key elements of this way of life. In particular you'll see that women are expected to—

- Take care of everyone else first.
- Be primarily responsible for cleaning house and cooking meals.
- Keep their bodies beautiful at all costs.
- Hold in strong emotions. Don't be angry. Pretend all is well.
- Submit, go along and let the boys win.

"Is Everyone Okay?"

Women are trained to take care of people. They are the relationship nurturers. They hold marriages and families together. That's a big job!

Part of this desire to take care of people is biological—there seems to be an inborn desire to nurture others. To the chagrin of some progressive parents, most little girls really do prefer playing with dolls to carrying a briefcase or operating a fire engine. Further, when you've had a baby grow inside of you and come through your body into the world, you look at that child differently than would a male. There is an attachment between mother and children that most fathers must work hard to even approach.

However, while some of the need to nurture is biological, most of it is learned behavior, taught by mothers and grandmothers and reinforced by important males in a woman's life. This desire to monitor and improve the relationship is so universal that it's led to a joke shared among my counselor friends. We have a saying: "If the man calls to initiate couple's therapy, it's probably too late!" That may sound cynical or sexist, but it's not. Let me explain how it happens.

Most often the woman has been saying, "We need help!" for a long time. She's seen the problems and attempted to talk about them. When that doesn't work, she suggests that they seek some assistance in dealing with their issues. The man resists by saying, "We can handle this." Or "I'm not telling our problems to a complete stranger!" So she suffers for a long time. Sometimes she endures the disappointment in silence; at other times she may be quite vocal. She continues to focus on making things better. But there comes a point when she gives up. When she's had all she can take, she tells her partner she doesn't feel the same love for him that she once did. Or she may say that she's through with the relationship altogether. It's at that point that he might say, "Wait! Let's try counseling." Then he calls a counselor and sets up an appointment. She may agree to go, but often her heart isn't in it. She would have tried and tried with enthusiasm a year or two or five earlier, but not now. She saw the problems a long time ago and she's worn out with working on them.

Many women in relationships give more than they get, hoping that at some point down the road the other person—spouse, partner, boss, friend or parent—will finally reciprocate. She may be so tired that she can't give any more, but still she struggles to give. Katherine gave more than she received for the first dozen years of her marriage. It was only in the last five years that she fully realized that Eddie wasn't even attempting to meet her needs. During this last half-decade of her marriage, she finally gave up her need to stay in the marriage while waiting for Eddie to match her willingness to give.

You may also recall the story of Edna in Chapter 2. She'd given all she could in her relationship with her adult son. She was tired and had little energy left for herself, yet her son continued to demand even more from her. She wanted to say no. Even then, her programming wouldn't allow her to stop. She'd been taught to take care of him no matter how she was being treated. There are few choices available to you when you hold this give-at-all-costs philosophy of life.

Do Women Have the Cooking and Cleaning Gene?

Pause a moment and take this simple test. A person is sitting in a comfortable chair in the living room. Suddenly, a hand is raised by the person in the chair, holding aloft a glass that is empty except for a few ice cubes in the bottom. With a shake of the wrist, the owner of the arm says, "Honey, I need a refill." Now quickly, guess the gender of the person in the chair. And see if you can identify the gender of the person being affectionately, yet self-servingly called, "Honey."

How did you do on this little test? Did you have any trouble identifying the two roles in this scenario? Probably not. You've seen it a hundred times at family dinners and holiday gatherings. You've no doubt heard it in your own den. You could call it The Tea Glass Syndrome.

Most of the time it's the woman of the house that has the primary responsibility for housekeeping and preparing meals. She might have the authority to ask her mate to stop at the store on his way home, but if she doesn't ask, he seldom notices that they are in need of milk or bread or toilet paper. Until they're out. Then he may notice in a rather gruff and noisy way.

"Excuse me," you might want to say, "but isn't this division of labor negotiable?" And of course the answer is, "Yes!" But you'll have to be the one to initiate the negotiations. If you're part of a typical couple, your partner is getting too much out of this to want to change, unless he's sensitive enough to see how tired or frustrated you're becoming.

Too many couples are still working with an old, stereotypical model which stipulates that the husband is primarily responsible for making a living and the wife keeps the house. That model may have worked better in the fifties when few wives worked outside the home. Today this formula is blatantly unfair to wives and mothers who are holding down a full-time job in addition to the housework they're responsible for. Healthy couples talk about how much they do around the house and if the division of labor seems unfair, they work to renegotiate. (By the way, when you start discussing who does what around the house, your partner may suggest that males don't have a take-out-the-trash or fix-the-car gene!)

"Sugar and Spice and Everything Nice"

The Body Beautiful

As I'm putting the finishing touches on this chapter, a popular women's magazine has arrived with a cover story on women and how they feel about their breasts. The answers indicate that a lot of women are very unhappy with their bodies, a "deep-rooted dislike—hatred, even" the author of the article says. In particular, most of the women who responded to the survey disliked the size and shape of their breasts. Some researchers believe that negative body image among women is more prevalent today than it ever has been in American life. We're having difficulty with the concept of seeing and accepting a woman as a whole person. We're slow to believe that she isn't defined by the physical package she arrives in.

The picture of beauty painted in our culture is difficult for women to live up to. Check most women's magazines and you'll find a tall, thin, blonde woman on the cover. Have you ever seen a heavy super-model? Claudia Schiffer is 5'11" and weighs in at a scant 112 pounds. That's thirty pounds underweight according to the chart in your doctor's office. The women on the covers of national magazines are promoted as the ideal, even though very few women have the genetic good fortune to be able to pull it off. With the exception of Roseanne Barr, female televisions characters are usually thin. Oprah Winfrey loses 70 pounds and becomes a national heroine. According to what you see in the media, thinness and success go hand in hand.

This view of what's considered beautiful isn't shared in every culture. For instance, I've read that in the days of Hawaiian royalty, the thinking about body image was much different than our current mentality. To be thin meant poverty; if you had no money to buy food, you'd eat less and obviously be thinner. The affluent, the well-to-do, were all heavy. Heftiness was a physical expression of the fact that you were wealthy. A Hawaiian queen would eat until she could eat no more, then servants would massage her stomach in order to speed up digestion so that she could eat again. This procedure would insure that the first lady was, by our standards, a fat lady.

If an emphasis on physical fitness is held within healthy bounds, it could promote a consciousness of beneficial diet and exercise patterns. However, if it's left unchecked, if being thin and looking good become an obsession, dangerous patterns develop. For many women, that's exactly what has happened. Being thin has become the only important goal.

Diets and diet-related aids are a $33 billion dollar a year industry in the U.S. And the failure rate on those diets is reported to be over

90%, so the supply of customers seeking new avenues to thinner living is never-ending.

Some women go to great extremes in their attempt to live up to the ideal. Anorexia and bulimia are two avenues some women travel in a vain attempt to arrive at their ideal weight. Never mind that such abuse breaks down a woman's immune system, damages muscle and organ tissue and can lead to chemical imbalances. To some people the only important consideration is, "You've lost how many pounds? That's great!" Such self-abuse is an expensive way to lose weight. And remember this: nine out of ten anorectics and bulimics are *female*. The pressure to live up to a particular body image falls heavier on women than on men.

If the only focus is being thin, a woman will give away her choices. How can she know what she wants and speak up to ask for it when she's living her life obsessed with a superficial presentation of herself? There is so much more to you than what you see when you look into the mirror, especially when the mirror is distorted by your culture's unrealistic expectations.

Barbie Dolls and Dream Houses

What is the cause of this craziness, this overemphasis on shape and size? Some writers would blame the media, sexist attitudes, or women's low self-esteem. I believe the answer is much simpler. I think this unrealistic view of what the ideal female body should look like has been caused primarily by one factor—the Barbie doll.

You think I'm kidding, don't you? Just think about it. Who would ever have thought that a toy could create such havoc? How can a eleven-inch tall sample of molded plastic be so destructive to the psyche of so many women? How in the world did Barbie become a national icon?

This doll seems to have summed up the American concept of the ideal woman. Tall and thin. Tiny feet and immaculate features. Perfect breasts and long blonde hair. No cellulite on her body. No wrinkles in her skin or bags under her eyes. In fact, she has no flaws anywhere to be seen.

Barbie has sold young women a view of the world that hinders a choice-filled life. Her flawless features perpetuate a cultural myth as to how a woman should look. "Beauty is only skin deep" the saying goes, but it seems to go much deeper in the case of this plastic beauty.

She lives in a dream house and drives a Corvette. She has lavish outfits and beautiful furniture. In the dream house she doesn't have a spatula or a frying pan. Can you imagine her vacuuming the rug? What, and ruin those nails?

She is made to be a perfect match for Ken, another real doll that any living male would have a difficult time matching in looks and build. However, in order to keep him, she'd better stay thin and fit. God knows that a perfect man deserves nothing but the best in the woman with whom he has a relationship.

No wonder you're left feeling inadequate. With that kind of role model, you'll never look good enough. If you're to have a choice-filled life, you'll have to find another role model. Absolute perfection isn't a goal we humans can attain.

Men Assert; Women Bitch?

I once read the summary of a well-planned and interesting research project. Male and female subjects were asked to watch two video tapes and rate the assertiveness and the appropriateness or inappropriateness of the actions of a man and a woman seen on the tape. The subjects didn't know this, but the actors on the screen were speaking *exactly the same words*, memorized from an identical script. First the tape showed a male, then a female, who had been wronged in a retail setting and were asking for the wrong to be made right. Both genders said the same words in much the same tone of voice. The results were interesting. Most of the men and women in the research project rated the male's responses as appropriate and assertive. However, most of the males and females alike rated the female's response as "bitchy" and inappropriate, even though in reality she was saying exactly the same words as the male.

This double standard isn't fair, but it's one of the dilemmas of being a female in our culture. You may have seen a T-shirt made for a woman to wear which reads in large letters: B.I.T.C.H.* The asterisk refers you to the bottom of the shirt where this word becomes an acronym—Being In Touch Creates Havoc. The message on this shirt implies, "Some people can't deal with me when I know what I want!" You're sometimes encouraged to be assertive, but if you're forceful in setting your boundaries, you may be labeled a "bitch."

If you're a female and you've been wronged, you're expected to smile sweetly and go on. Just pretend that all is well. "No problem here!"

You're encouraged not to be angry. If you feel angry, you're taught just to file it away. Of course this leads to a stack of resentments the size of a small office building, but that's the way you're told you must respond. Following such expectations will of course empty your reserve tank. Look again at Chapter 6 if you aren't yet convinced of the importance of feeling and responding to *all* your emotions.

Let the Boys Win

When I was in graduate school we worked with a family whose presenting problem was the falling grades of the twelve year old daughter. She'd done well throughout elementary school, making A's in most of her classes since the first grade. As she entered junior high she was suddenly doing poorly on material that mom and dad were sure she knew. They came in as a family in an attempt to understand what was happening.

As a part of our initial interview, my co-therapist and I talked with the young woman alone. I suppose what we found out shouldn't have been shocking, but I was taken by surprise because I'd never heard it before. She told us that she'd recently started going steady with a boy in her class and she didn't want to leave him feeling bad by making better grades than he did. She was throwing the tests intentionally, answering questions incorrectly when she knew the right answers. In this way she was purposely giving him the edge when test scores were announced. This made complete sense to her. The only real problem she saw herself as having was that her parents and her teachers were disappointed in her work and didn't think she was applying herself. "They just wouldn't understand," she said. Sadly, I'm afraid some women might understand all too well.

This young lady had learned early a message that has crippled many women: Let the men win. Give in to their demands. Don't damage their fragile egos. Let them be in charge, or at least let them think they're in charge. Don't be real. Don't make demands. Serve your husband. If you don't, it reflects poorly on him and on you. Those rules will have to be challenged if you're to live a life full of choices.

Sometimes this expectation that men are to have their way is cloaked in religious jargon and called "submission." To some people, submission seems to mean that women have to park their brains and forgo their own wills in order to be happily married. I don't believe that's the model for womanhood the Bible portrays.

You can scarcely attend a wedding ceremony in which the minister doesn't read Paul's famous words from Ephesians chapter five which describe the appropriate interplay of married couples. In all honesty, Paul does use the word "submission," but it's clear that this act of submitting isn't to be a one-way street. His description involves mutual submission—wives to husbands and husbands to wives. Whatever submission means, the road goes in both directions.

Many couples need to rethink their concept of submission. When it's mentioned in the Bible at all, it's something that a husband and a wife are called to accept, not something that can be forced upon a spouse by his or her partner. Further, a husband is called by Scripture to give more than he expects from his wife. He's to find ways to outgive her, if you will, when it comes to their marital relationship. Finally, when you look at other Bible passages, it is clear that women are equal to men and are to be treated with the dignity belonging to equals. (See Galatians 3:28.)

Too Busy for Choices

Women have long been charged with making the home and family run smoothly. However, recently I've been seeing a new wrinkle that's been added to the equation. While many men have long used their career as a way to cope with pain in their lives or as a way to escape the intensity of an intimate relationship, more and more often I'm hearing the same story from women. Many women are now working those long days and stress-filled hours away from home that were once the hallmark of males in our culture.

Catrina was a single woman of 38 who worked in management in the health care field. Downsizing had led to her having more to do with less support people to assist her. She came to see me because she knew that her work had gotten out of control. She put in 12-hour days with regularity five days a week, then would go to her office for a few hours on Saturday and Sunday so she could catch up on work before starting the next week.

She was so tired that she could only sit on the couch when she got home at night. She had little energy to clean house, engage in a hobby or even go for a walk. She seldom called or spent time with friends. Mostly she just settled into a daze on the sofa, cuddling with her cat. She would fall asleep on the couch, then at some point during the night drag herself to bed. The next morning she would take a hot shower and tank up on coffee in an effort to invigorate herself, then start the entire workday routine over again.

One day, though, she was too tired to make it to work. She was completely exhausted. She'd ignored the falling level in her reserve tank for so long that her body and emotions now screamed for attention. In fact, she was so tired that when she called me to make an appointment, she wanted to schedule it two days later because she said she was too tired to come in. She needed some time to recharge her batteries first.

In Chapter 17 you'll learn more about why you work the way you do and what you need to do to place work into a healthy perspective in your life. For our purposes here, note that a woman can let work get out of hand when she—

1. Uses her job to take the place of a relationship with a man or close friends.

2. Uses work to escape from herself, hiding her pain or regret in a flurry of activity.

3. Wants appreciation and attention so badly she'll work hour after hour in the hopes that she'll receive it though her boss, her co-workers and her paycheck.

4. Has such poor boundaries that she can't say no to the requests of her boss or manager, accumulating more and more items on her list of workday duties.

In Catrina's case, all four of these played a part. She had a difficult time making changes in any of these areas, much less all of them, but slowly she was able to do so. The thought that became her compass was this: I am finite and I can't do it all. Where do I need to draw the line?

The Dream Dies Hard

It's difficult to give up thoughts of princes and castles and waking up to his kiss after a long night spent in a death sleep. It's more fun to imagine a fairy godmother who will rescue you from the mundane than it is to continue to live in and struggle with your current, less-than-princely circumstances.

But coming back to reality has to happen if you're to live a choice-filled life. Life isn't a fairy tale and no matter how hard you try, you don't live happily ever after. Even the best relationship is hard work. Accepting that view of reality is central to the process of regaining your power to choose.

Letting go of the dream of a magical existence is difficult, but necessary to the growth process. Be forewarned that the dream dies hard. It's so pervasive, it touches all aspects of your life. You literally can be intoxicated by the fantasy. Over the years, you'll either relinquish the fantasy's hold on you or you'll have to expend more effort to cover the pain you've been working so hard to avoid by living in that dream world.

You can't continue to live in a world of pretend if you want to be genuine. Only when you see yourself and your relationships for what they really are can you make healthy and effective choices.

It may sound like I'm asking you to give up something valuable for something that's not very exciting and which promises lots of hard work. What I'm really suggesting is that you give up an impossible dream for a marvelous reality. I'm encouraging you to stop living on cotton candy—which tastes sweet and may give you a sense of having eaten something special—because it can't meet your nutritional needs. Instead, live on vegetables and healthy grains which can satisfy your hunger and meet your body's needs for fuel to accomplish it's many tasks.

Most women have to hit bottom before things can begin to change. For some women, the dream only dies when the man in her life leaves her, when she suffers from excruciating physical pain, when she becomes so depressed she can't go on, or when she or the man in her life has an affair. If you can be real through this, if you can grieve the loss of a misguided ideal and move on to reality, a new and satisfying way of life can be yours.

The answer isn't to be found in men-bashing. Unloading on the man or men in your life when you've had all you can stand doesn't help. There's just no future in that negative approach. Besides, men don't gain from the traditional organization of roles either. That will be more clearly laid out in the next chapter. Instead of blaming men or your mother or our culture, the way to change is to empower yourself. Accept the truth that you can make your own decisions! You can question the rules. You can learn to listen to yourself. Give yourself permission to look for alternatives. Allow yourself to experience fully your personal power to choose.

This is the very process that Katherine, the woman whose story opened this chapter, went through. After the divorce, she went to counseling and to Al-Anon. She spent a lot of time taking a personal inventory. She took responsibility for the problems in the marriage that were her fault. She grew by leaps and bounds in this atmosphere of personal exploration and acceptance.

The journey toward a choice-filled life wasn't a straight line for her. She made some significant mistakes in the process. She once again tried some fairy tale relationships, looking for someone to rescue her and the children. But she continued to focus on herself and as she did so, she let go of the concept of finding someone else who could make life better for her. She grew stronger and felt at peace with herself. Only then could she look in the right places to find the man she later married.

Six years after her divorce, she remarried and is happier than she's ever been. For the first time in her adult life, she's living in reality instead of in a dream. She has her choices, speaks up to voice what she wants (most of the time), and has found a partner who's willing to do the same.

In the process, she challenged a lot of her old expectations. Katherine is now following a revised model of what it means to be a woman. She's not smarter or more talented than you are. You can make these changes, too. Katherine changed when she was tired of what she was getting out of life. She changed when she was ready to change. Remember:

If you continue to do what you've always done,
you'll continue to get the same outcome.

POWER TO CHOOSE: In what ways does your role as a woman need to be changed?

_____

_____

_____

_____

Are you ready to make those changes? Explain.

_____

_____

_____

_____

10

WHAT'S A "REAL MAN" ANYWAY?
Creating a New Map for Masculinity

THE FACTS ARE PLAIN: the average life-span of a man is seven or eight years shorter than for a woman. Men suffer more ulcers and heart attacks. Men are going to doctors, psychiatrists and counselors with complaints of depression more often than in the past.

What's at the core of the early death, physical complaints and the growing awareness of emotional pain? While a part of the explanation may be genetic, a major portion of the problem is the very role that men have been asked to play. The definition of masculinity that you've accepted has affected your ability to exercise your power to choose. Years of following a warped definition of manhood has resulted in empty tanks and dissatisfying lives. This kind of life takes a heavy toll emotionally and physically. Continuing to follow these rules will result in more of the same. Nothing changes unless you change the principles which underlie the problems.

Physical, emotional and relationship problems due to depleting roles.

For many of you, it's time to rethink your definition of masculinity. What's a "real man" anyway? How should a man behave? How are you supposed to treat the women in your life? What are you to do with your emotions? What does it mean to truly be a man?

What Does it Mean to be a Man?

Aaron was a newcomer to the men's group. He was obviously tense and ill at ease. He found it difficult to be still, fidgeting with his coat or his hands. His glance darted away from any direct eye contact with the other men in the circle. He admitted he was nervous about being present and felt one down to the other men who made up the group. "I look at all of you," he said, "And feel inadequate because I know that you all know how to be men and I don't!" As the discussion moved from man to man around the room, almost all of them responded to Aaron's comment. Most of them said the same thing: "We may cover it better than you do, but we're wrestling with the same thing. We also want to know: What does it mean to be a man?"

Most men I know who feel comfortable being honest about it will admit that they don't feel confident that they understand what the script for manhood calls for, much less that they are playing it out effectively in their own lives. Most of you probably feel the same way. This fear of not measuring up is covered up or denied in any number of ways, but it's ever-present. You can sense an overwhelming feeling of failure or fatigue when you listen to men talk about their attempts to live up to society's conception of manhood.

What does a normal man do? For many men, "normal" is working 75 hours a week, having no close relationships with anyone but your mate (and not being very close to her), and spending less than 30 minutes a day with your children. It's criticizing your sports team, government and government officials. It's eating too much too fast while getting little exercise. It includes a diet of too much coffee, too much sugar and very little that's healthy.

Many men are realizing how this recipe for manhood has resulted in a very poor cake. You may have thought you mismeasured the ingredients or that you misread the directions, so you've been trying it over and over to see if you could get a better outcome. But every time you try it, you get a bad cake. It's time for a new recipe!

Where do you go to learn the rules which tell you how to be a man? What do you do when you feel like you don't measure up? And on top of it all, there's that gnawing question: will the role of manhood you've been taught to perform lead you to the satisfaction you want from life? It seems the answer to that last question is, "No."

Where did you learn how to be a man? What school did you attend to get your education? Where did you do your apprenticeship? Most of you have a problem because the men in your life weren't there to

What's a "Real Man" Anyway?

show you how to be a man when you were younger. Most of you were raised by women. You spent most of your school-aged years with mothers and grandmothers, aunts and sisters. The men were gone to work, gone to play at their favorite gym, golf course or fishing hole, or spending time drinking at their favorite "watering hole." You had no model for what genuine manhood looks like. One lesson you did learn was that being a man meant being gone.

Some of you had fathers who did come home, but when they did they still weren't really there. Your dad was hung over, strung out, or burnt out. Many fathers who came home spent the bulk of their evening working in the yard or in the garage or vegged out in front of the television. You learned that being a man meant being physically present, but emotionally absent.

At the other extreme, some of you were raised by men who were attempting to be a clone of Ward Cleaver. You thought that in order to be a man, you were supposed to be perpetually available to meet the needs of others. Problems were supposed to be easily and neatly solved. Communication never resulted in a ruckus. No one got angry and if he or she did, it was never very passionate. Even the mildest argument was to be avoided. You felt compelled to apologize profusely for any attempt to express your vantage point. You learned that men should be quiet and resourceful and that they always solve problems quickly. How much different than reality! Life is *not* easy and problems often continue for days or weeks.

You've been at a loss because you wanted more from your father than he gave you, and you wanted to be able to give more to the people who are important to you. But you didn't know how to be a man in a different way. You learned the model your father showed you and while you don't really believe it was very healthy, you haven't known how else to behave. If he was absent physically or emotionally, you probably have been, too. You missed your dad and wanted him to be a bigger part of your life. You swore you'd be a different spouse and parent yourself, yet you find yourself doing what dad did. You spend your life hiding behind your work, your hobbies, your wife, or a bottle. If your approach was to solve the problems for everyone in the family, they no doubt perceived you as meddlesome or controlling.

Your heroes were men like John Wayne, James Bond and Rambo. You aspired to be playboys, war heroes and sports legends because you thought they had what you didn't—a sense of purpose, power to control their lives, an air of success, and plenty of perfect women.

The whole picture is sadly false and has led to tank-emptying behavior and chronically low reserve tank levels.

Following false heros leads to empty tanks.

Learning from the Media

In the vacuum of a model for meaningful manhood, the media has stepped in to sell you their concept of what real men look like. While there are some exceptions, most movies and television programs portray the masculine role as one of emotional and physical distancing, failure to communicate and constant sexual conquest. You've been to the media school of manhood and learned from television fathers like Archie Bunker, Ben Cartwright, and Clint Hukstable. You've watched the sexual exploits of Sam Malone on *Cheers* and Hawkeye Pierce in *M*A*S*H*. You've wanted to be able just once to introduce yourself as, "Bond. James Bond," and have it be true! Movies and television, *Playboy* and *Penthouse*, even the machismo applauded in the news have led you to believe that real men are promiscuous, beer drinking sports nuts who put down their wives and criticize their children.

To compensate for your failing sense of masculinity, many advertisers encourage you to buy their products. The often all too clear message is that unless you buy what they're selling, you're inferior. Without their wares you're nobody; with them you can be somebody! "Do you doubt your masculinity?" the ads seem to say. "Then buy our car (or clothes or beer or cologne or deodorant) and you'll feel secure and successful!" And you respond! Because of your doubts and fears that you're not measuring up, you line up to buy what they're selling.

Catch phrases stereotype men and attempt to dictate what they should or shouldn't be:
- Real men don't eat quiche!
- Don't let them see you sweat!
- You only go around once in life, so grab all the gusto you can!
- Never back down from a fight.
- Boys don't play with dolls.
- Men don't cry.

Of course none of these are true. Of course none of these are healthy ways to live. Of course no one believes these. Or do they?

A Ken and Barbie World?

Trent was visibly upset when he arrived for his counseling session on Thursday. It was obvious that something was troubling him deeply. The counselor greeted him, then waited for him to speak.

Trent took a moment to gather his thoughts. "I've realized something about myself that's hard to admit," he began. "I've been duped!" he exclaimed. "I've bought the media's idea of what 'ideal' men and women should look like and how they should behave.

"Physically, they're supposed to be young and flawless. Wrinkles and imperfect bodies are unacceptable. 'Old' is to be feared, not revered.

"At work, no one should see you sweat. You're supposed to handle every challenge with conspicuous ease.

"Everyone should look good, even first thing in the morning when they wake up. And no one smells offensive because there are deodorants and colognes that cover odors and will make you appealing to the opposite sex. Mouthwash takes care of stale breath.

"Neat, clean, perfect. That's the way the world is supposed to be.

"I've been having problems with relationships for years. I think I'm beginning to understand where some of the problems come from. What I've been looking for in a relationship is someone to play Barbie to my Ken. Two perfect specimens of humanity who are flawless in form, emotion, and behavior.

"But, of course, I've known that it's not like that. The only way things can appear to be so tidy is for you to deny the way things really are.

"I knew I couldn't be Ken and felt the failure of that imperfection. But I still wanted her to be Barbie! My desire for perfection has kept me from accepting the beauty of the relationships I've had in my grasp."

Many of you bought it. This is the way you thought the world was supposed to be. Those women in *Playboy* are available for you and they are capable of deep and lasting relationships! If you use Old Spice and floss, you'll be happily involved with the woman of your choice. Bikini ski teams made up of D cup women are waiting for you, if you'll only drink the right beer or carry the correct credit card!

Television and movies are a major source of information about your world, but the view of reality they present is skewed. When you watch an event on TV, even the worst pictures imaginable can be cleaned up, distanced from you and sanitized. TV shows get into and out of problems in 30 minutes. Happy endings are easy. Smiles seem warm and genuine even on days when actors have headaches. Garbage dumps or chemical spills don't smell on TV. Wrinkles can be removed. Special lenses make women look younger, softer and more appealing. Love scenes are rehearsed to perfection, filmed over a series of days, then condensed to only a few minutes of viewing time. Your life can't measure up to what you see presented in the media.

It may make you feel better temporarily to buy the sanitized view of life that the media presents, but it's not reality. The reality is that life is a struggle. People wake up unkempt and with bad breath. All of us age and wrinkle. The physical condition of your body or the body of your partner has little to do with how happy your life will be. Sex doesn't always go well. Happy endings exist only in fairy tales.

The media has sold you a bill of goods! What they present as reality isn't. But if their picture isn't true, then what is? What's a real man?

Where are the Real Men?

Are there any real men? I believe there are, but you won't always find them where you thought you would. You have to look closely to be able to see them.

Real men are just that: they're real. They're genuine. They can feel their emotions and respond appropriately. They set limits with other people, yet do so without withdrawing from them. They're able to make healthy connection with others without losing themselves. They have a strong sense of self and can separate themselves from others.

Real men seek to be honest in their relationships with themselves, their friends and family and relatives. Simply put, they tell the truth. They don't lie about anything. They don't even tell little white lies.

What's a "Real Man" Anyway?

They don't have to say everything that pops into their head, but neither do they hide themselves behind any hint of falsehood.

Real men accept the different aspects of themselves and honor them all. They're able to value the part of themselves that makes provision for all the people in their world, the part that sets limits, the part that can see the mystical and magical and can solve even complex problems and the part that allows them to see the beautiful and romantic in the world and in other people. Real men know all these facets and seek to be balanced in their expression of them.

Real men don't have to be right. They can be wrong and admit it when they are. They don't have to prove they're right when they're having an argument because they've realized that both parties think they're right or they wouldn't be having the fight in the first place. Real men believe that it's less important to be right than it is to be real. Helpful problem-solving can begin when the people with the problem risk being real.

Real men can listen. They hear what other people say to them. They seek first to understand, then to be understood. They believe that if men would do this one thing with their girlfriends and spouses, friends and acquaintances, and employees and co-workers, their relationships would immediately change for the better.

Real men can talk. They express their needs, which implies that they've taken inventory and know what those needs are. Real men are willing to take the risk to ask for what they want. At the same time, they're willing to let the answer to their request be "No." (Remember that when you ask for something, if the other person doesn't have the right to say, "No," it's not a request, it's an order!)

Real men can touch and be touched. The side of them that loves life and loves people comes out in the form of physical expression. They can be tender. They hug their children and their wives. They're even learning to hug their male friends!

Real men know that making love involves more than breasts and genitals. They touch their spouse or lover in many ways at many times of the day, not just when they're ready for intercourse. They've learned that knees and shoulders and feet can be erogenous zones. They've experienced the excitement of giving or receiving a hand massage, a back rub, or kissing for twenty minutes. They're growing more and more comfortable with touching and being touched.

Real men can listen with an empathetic heart. Other people can approach them without fear of being hurt, put down, or shamed. They care about the feelings of others.

Real men can also stand tough. They can defend their boundaries. They can draw a line and say, "Don't come past here unless you're willing to do battle!" They don't violate the boundaries of others, nor do they allow others to violate their limits. They don't look for an argument, but they don't flinch from one either.

These real men are men of choice. They can feel the strength of their power to choose. Because they're aware of their emotions and possible choices and because they're careful not to violate the choices of others, they're able to live satisfying, full tank lives:

Following new roles allows the tank to be filled.

Courage to Change

Your tank will continue to be emptied until you begin to follow a different set of rules as to what it means to be a man. If you want your life to be richer, you'll have to take charge. And if things are to change, you'll have to be willing to face your own fears. You've been afraid to trust, afraid to be honest, afraid that you won't measure up to the expectations of the role of masculinity that you've been asked to play. Those fears have to be faced. You can't wait until all the apprehension is gone. Feel the fear and act anyway! Act now. Take steps to change your life.

You can't just rearrange the furniture and change the way you're living. The entire house has to be remodeled! Here are some suggestions to assist you in making changes.

1. Change begins when you're **willing to risk**. It takes great courage to challenge the concept of manhood that your father, your friends and your co-workers may still be following. You may hear other men say, "You're pussy-whipped!" because you listen to your mate. You may be thought a wimp if you cease to bully other people. You'll have to be absolutely convinced of the need for change before

you'll have the necessary energy to make the changes and maintain them.

2. It's essential to **get honest**. Be genuine with yourself and those with whom you have relationships. Tell the truth. Avoid even little white lies. Ask yourself how you feel and respond to the answer you hear. If your tank is growing empty, take action immediately to alter the situation. Remember that even minor adjustments to what is going into and out of your tank can result in a significant difference in the level of your emotional reserve tank.

3. **Find a supportive man or group of men** to talk to. Talking to women can help, but talking with men is absolutely essential. You'll find it encouraging, perhaps even amazing, to see how many men are feeling just like you. Honest conversation with other men allows you to say out loud what you're struggling with and what you want to change. You'll find the answers to your dilemma of living the life of a real man by spending time in the world of men.

You don't know of a group? You can't wait to discover a support network. It's time to act. Get serious about finding a group. You may want to start one of your own. It can be a group of friends, men from your church, or men you work with.

4. **Remember your power of choice**. You have the power to feel, to express your feelings, to be imperfect and to be yourself. Use those choices to change your life.

Much of what you've been taught about being a man is learned behavior, not ingrained heredity. If you change the behavior, you can change your life. Change the way you think and you change your very definition of manhood.

After years of eating a dissatisfying cake, it's time to try something new!

POWER TO CHOOSE: Describe one thing that is changing in your concept of what it means to be a man.

_____

_____

_____

_____

11

THERE'S NO SUCH THING AS "HAD TO!"
Generating Alternative Choices

ONE THING that will keep you stuck and deplete your tank is *not* seeing the choices you have. Often the first step toward change is seeing that you *do* have a choice. Usually you have several choices. This chapter is designed to help you generate additional choices.

Listen to the traps in the following quotes. See if you can see yourself in any of these—

- "I was so angry about being forced to go to his mother's house again last weekend. We seem to go there *every* Sunday. Just once I'd like to have Sunday to myself so that I could do what I wanted to do. But I *had* to go with him. I had no choice!"
- "I'm sorry, Professor Martin, but I have to miss your class on Thursday. You see, I'm on the university golf team and we have a tournament in Rockford and I have to be there. I have no choice."
- "But dad, all the other kids dared me to jump! I didn't want to be a wimp, so I did it. I had to! I had no choice!"
- "I really wanted the blue blazer, but the black was all they had left. I bought it anyway. I had no choice."
- "I didn't really want to work late on Friday night, but the boss asked me to stay to complete the Peterson deal. I hated to cancel out on the plans I'd made with Sue and the kids, but I had to. I had no choice."

How many times have you heard yourself say something similar? "I had no choice!" It sounds powerful sometimes. It may deflect the criticism or objections of others. But "I had no choice" is just not a true statement. There may be consequences to other choices that you'd prefer not to experience, but you always have a choice!

- Wives don't *have* to go their mother-in-law's every Sunday afternoon. They can negotiate with their husbands. They can express their desire for something else.
- College students on the golf team don't *have* to go to the tournaments. Of course, not going would probably mean discipline or dismissal from the team, so an athlete who wanted to remain on the team would probably go. But he or she doesn't *have* to do so.
- Your children do lots of things as a response to peer pressure. The power of a dare is so universal that it's an integral part of the story line in the "Back to the Future" movies. Marty can't stand to be called "chicken," so he does what he feels pressured to do to meet the challenges of others. But it doesn't *have* to be that way. Marty finally figures that out.
- You don't *have* to buy a black blazer when you wanted a blue one. You may choose to buy a black one because you want a new blazer or because it's on sale or because you need a blazer to wear to a function. But you don't *have to* buy it.
- The "have to's" of work aren't as absolute as you've made them sound. An entire chapter will be dedicated to exploring the issue of work. (See Chapter 17.) For now, note that you have choices at work just as you have choices in the rest of your life. You don't *have to* work late.

If you believe you don't have a choice, you'll feel trapped. If you believe that there's only one option available to you, you'll tend to resent it. What you must see in order to exercise your freedom of choice is that you're *always* choosing from among many choices. Only then can you take back your personal power.

You always have a choice! None of your choices may be very appealing. Honestly, there are times when your best choice is one of several poor choices. But you still have a choice. One choice may stand out as being easier, less stressful, more pragmatic, or less problematic, but that doesn't make it your only choice.

When you say, "I had no choice," you give up your power to choose. You fail to sense the power you have. Your tank is emptied a little or a lot. Only when you take back your power can you realize your potential.

The more you see new possibilities for the various aspect of your world, the more adaptive you'll be. You'll take back more of your power to choose. Often you're limited not by the boundaries of your world, but by the limits of your own failure to see options. Your

There's No Such Thing as "Had To!"

Depleter: giving choices to others.

inability to see options won't just limit your choices; the failure to see options can lead you to believe that you *have* no choices. This is a sure way to give away your power of choice. Control of your tank is turned over to others.

Possibility Thinking

In order to generate more choices, you'll have to plug in to your creative self. You'll need to exercise your ability to engage in possibility thinking. Possibility thinking is like coloring outside the lines. It's freeing your mind to think of things in new and different ways.

Have you ever pretended that a pencil was a drum stick? Have you used a clothes pin to close an opened bag of potato chips? Have you scratched your back with a long wooden spoon? If you've done any of these, or anything like them, you've been using your ability to think of possibilities.

Try to solve this puzzle using your possibility thinking. Without lifting the pen from the paper and only making four straight lines, connect all the dots in the follow diagram. (You'll find the solution later on in this chapter.)

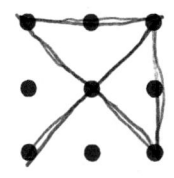

Use the right-brained, more unstructured part of yourself. Think more like a child. Children can be so creative when they play. A paper towel roll becomes a telescope. A plastic bowl is a flying saucer. The dog can be dressed up to become a favorite friend. Stuffed bears hear profound secrets. As you grow older, it's easy to lose this ability to see possibilities for what's around you. Your sense of the novel begins to die. When this happens, you lose some of your choices.

You're classifying things continuously: that's a red sweater, this is a truck, there's a dog. Often you won't even be conscious of the process, but you're constantly sifting what you perceive into this or that pigeonhole. In many ways this can be beneficial. Someone may say, "Do you have the key?" and you know exactly what he's referring to. However, this process of putting things into categories can hurt you or those around you if the categories become so rigid that new possibilities are missed.

The more you see new possibilities for the various aspect of your world, the more adaptive you'll be. Often you're limited not by the boundaries of your world, but by your failure to see alternatives. This failure to see options won't just limit your choices, it can even leave you believing you have no choices.

The process of generating choices is energized through the process of possibility thinking. In order to sense more fully your personal power, it's vital to stay current and challenge yourself to think of things in new and useful ways.

You can get stuck when you hold fast to old or traditional ways of seeing things. Perhaps you've heard the story of the woman who always cut off the end of her holiday ham before she cooked it. When her husband asked her why she did this, she answered, "Because my mother did." When they called to ask the mother why she always cut off the end of the ham, she said that she'd done it that way because her mother had. A call to the grandmother revealed that she'd done so because her pan was too short. Even though the granddaughter's pan was plenty large for the entire ham, she'd continued to follow an inherited pattern.

The early automobiles were created around the design of the horse-drawn carriages that had preceded them. "Horseless carriage" was more than a descriptive term. It was an expression of the limitation that automobile designers put upon themselves. As the thinking changed that dictated cars had to look like carriages, the designs manufacturers used began to change.

Gathering New Data

Often you'll need new data in order to see alternative choices. Openness to new information helps keep you growing and fresh. Communication is to your emotional and relationship health what blood is to the body. It's essential. The flow of information feeds you and cleanses you. Without it, you'll die. New information keeps you thriving. Reading, going to seminars, listening to tapes and talking to others open the door to fresh input.

It's not uncommon for you to become so comfortable with the familiar that you don't notice changes that occur around you. Your mind can be placed on automatic pilot. New information is missed. For instance, read the following familiar quote:

A bird in the the hand is worth two in the bush.

Unless you've seen this little trick before or unless you're a suspicious person by nature, you probably didn't notice the two "the's" in the sentence. It's easy to assume you know what's going to be said and miss seeing something different.

As I've worked on this manuscript, I've had this point driven home to me repeatedly. Because I know what I expect a certain sentence or paragraph to say, it's difficult to edit my own work. As I read through what I've read, there are times when I supply words that aren't on the page because I know what I intended to say. An objective editor is essential to the successful completion of this project.

Parents can get stuck because they don't seek new information. When you parent your children, you may have used spanking as the only form of discipline. It was probably the one your parents most commonly used as a means of shaping your behavior. But there are many other choices, many of which work more effectively than spanking and which create much less tension and resentment than spanking. Discipline could also include time out, loss of privileges or the use of a point system which rewards positive behavior. Before new possibilities can be explored, old categories have to be challenged.

Alternative Interpretations

There are various possible interpretations for any act, fact or occurrence. You'll remember from the discussion in Chapter 5 that what happens has to be interpreted before you can respond to it. Meaning is attached to the things that happen to you. One way of experiencing your power to choose to find alternative explanations for what's going on in your world.

There are always multiple interpretations of events and facts. Some interpretations are more useful than others. Some are more "true" than others. But many exist. In order to reclaim choices, you'll need to open up the door to new possibilities.

Picture this scene. A mother and her four-year-old son are walking through the mall. The mother has insisted that her son hold her hand so he won't get lost. After about an hour of shopping, her son becomes cranky and continually attempts to pull his hand away. The mother interprets this behavior as disobedience and spanks her son. An alternative explanation might be that after an hour of reaching up, the boy's arm has fallen asleep. Because the boy doesn't know what's going on, he can't explain his discomfort to his parent. Instead, he simply attempts to get his arm down.

Your employee finally finishes a project he's been working on for a month. The quality of the work isn't up to his usual standards. You could interpret this as laziness, but there could be a number of other explanations. Perhaps he's distracted by problems at work or at home. A physical ailment may explain his inadequate performance. If you're open to other interpretations, you'll be better able to address the problem.

Did you figure out a solution to the 9 dot problem? A solution is shown below. The key is in seeing options! Don't let yourself be limited by the perimeter of the puzzle. In fact the only way to solve the puzzle is to go outside the lines. Be open to alternatives!

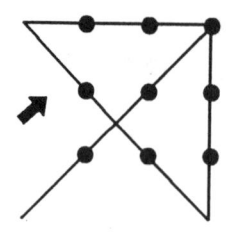

Rules Which Inhibit Seeing Choices

There are a number of rules which, when followed, can result in the lessening of your power to choose. If you're to take back your power of choice and raise the level of your reserve tank, these rules will have to be challenged. Let's discuss some of the more common of these troublesome rules.

Don't be selfish. Many of you have been taught to put the feelings and needs of others before your own. If you ask for what you need, you may feel guilty. It may seem selfish to think of doing for yourself.

Shawn thought that she had to do for others. Actually, to say she'd thought about it implies too much. She learned in her family that one way to get approval from her mother was to take care of things for her. Mom loved it when she cleaned house for her or offered to help with dinner. When she had a family of her own, it became automatic for her to think of what her husband or children needed before she thought of what she wanted for herself.

The problem with spending all your energy on others is that you have none left for yourself. Soon your depleted tank is too empty to meet the demands of life. You lose any healthy sense of yourself. You diminish your *personal power to choose*.

Don't make waves! One of the core concepts of family therapy is the concept of homeostasis. "Homeostasis" is defined as the tendency of a system to maintain equilibrium. Forces that call for change and forces that would elicit sameness cooperate to create stability. This constant movement allows for change in response to new input from inside or outside of the family.

In some families, change is looked upon as being bad. "Don't make waves" is the credo, whether it's directly stated or not. They may look good, but there's no sense of life. They're like a slide under a microscope—interesting to observe but dead as a hammer.

"Don't make waves!" means, "Follow the rules!" Do things the way they've always been done. Stifle creativity. Don't investigate new and alternative approaches. Tradition is better than innovation. If you're to regain your choices, some waves are inevitable.

You should be able to endure this. "What's the matter? Are you a sissy?" "You're always complaining." "Hey, if you can't stand the heat, get out of the kitchen!" "Just suck it up!"

Your job asks more and more of you, but you can't complain. You've got to be strong enough to handle the pressure. Your marriage is difficult, but you can't think of getting out. You've got to tough it out! Do you remember that story about the researchers who put a frog in some water? If you place a frog in hot water, he'll jump right out. If you put him in cool water and gradually turn up the heat, he'll literally cook. The increase in temperature sneaks up on him until he's well-done.

You need to be able to say, "Ouch!" or "This is too much!" When you're feeling overwhelmed, you must take the freedom to say so. Your choices will be minimized if you feel you can't do so.

Watch carefully for any statements that have "should" in them. Most of the time, should is a shame word. It's a stick you use to beat yourself up. "I should have gone the other way!" doesn't help. It only makes you feel worse about you. "Should" is a word that paralyzes. It shames you, passing judgment on your actions and intentions. No word is more devastating to your power to choose.

Don't let them know they got to you. What a summary statement of male machismo! Don't you be weak, now. Don't flinch. You flinch, I have to punish you. The first one who blinks loses. This rule is often fostered in homes where physical and emotional abuse were present. You may have learned to completely detach from your own feelings in order to deal with the abuse.

Saying you're hurt when you *are* hurting is like smiling when you're happy and tearing up when you're sad. They're all normal outward expressions of what you're feeling inside. To stuff that natural expression is to lose a part of yourself.

God wouldn't like it! While I do believe it's important to follow a moral code that shapes your behavior, you can't *not* feel the way you feel just because you've been told God might not like it. It seems to me that God is much less concerned than many Christians seem to be about the keeping of a few rules, chosen at random as being the most important ones.

Even if you believe that God wouldn't like the way you're feeling or the way you behave, denial of your emotions or needs isn't a healthy answer to dealing with the situation. Read the Psalms and notice how many days David had horrible things to say about himself and his view of God and his wishes that bad things would happen to people around him. My personal favorite is Psalm 109 in which David wishes harm on a man who'd hurt him. "Make his wife a widow and his children fatherless," the psalmist writes. "Kill him, God." Not a very loving thought, but that's where David was that day. (Do notice that David didn't take it on himself to hurt the man, but he did express his frustration.)

You Can Fly!

You can do things differently. Your life doesn't have to look the way it does right now. You have more options than you have exercised so far. Be creative. Look for new answers to old problems.

There's No Such Thing as "Had To!"

Explore new ways to look at your situation. Remember: there's no such thing as "had to"!

POWER TO CHOOSE: I love this piece by the philosopher Apollinaire. Use it as an occasion to reflect on the possibilities that can be yours if you'll only let go.

> "COME TO THE EDGE."
> "No, we will fall."
> "COME TO THE EDGE."
> "No, we will fall."
> They came to the edge.
> He pushed them, and they flew.

PART THREE

HEALING THE WOUNDS

12

PLUGGING THE LEAKS
Healing the Reserve Tank

WHEN YOU WERE BORN, you didn't yet have your reserve tank. Inside of you there was all the potential for a healthy and solid tank, but that potential needed to be nurtured. Creating an atmosphere in which your tank can develop properly is one of the important functions provided by your parents.

A useful and healthy tank can only be formed in a setting of acceptance, open communication and unconditional love. To whatever degree the home you grew up in was without these, to that degree will your tank be damaged.

If your tank wasn't developed in an environment which provided the incubation you needed to have a healthy tank, there will be weak places in the walls of your tank. These holes will allow the emotional energy in your tank to run out. Like a bucket that has rusted through, your tank won't be able to hold the emotional energy you collect within it. Some of your energy will be drained away.

A leaking tank allows emotional energy to escape.

Drip, drip, drip! Fast or slowly, but always consistently, energy is leaked from your tank. For some of you, the leak is so bad that it takes constant effort to have even the slightest bit of reserve. You have to work extremely hard just to have a small amount of energy available.

In addition, if your boundaries were violated by physical, sexual or emotional abuse, or if you weren't taught that you had the power to choose to say yes and no, the valves on your tank will also be damaged or disabled. It may appear to you that the other people in your life have more power to dictate how and when you use your energy than you do.

Healthy tanks don't have these weak places. They're completely and soundly formed so that the energy that goes into them is available for your use. Emotional energy goes into the tank and remains there until it flows through the depletion line.

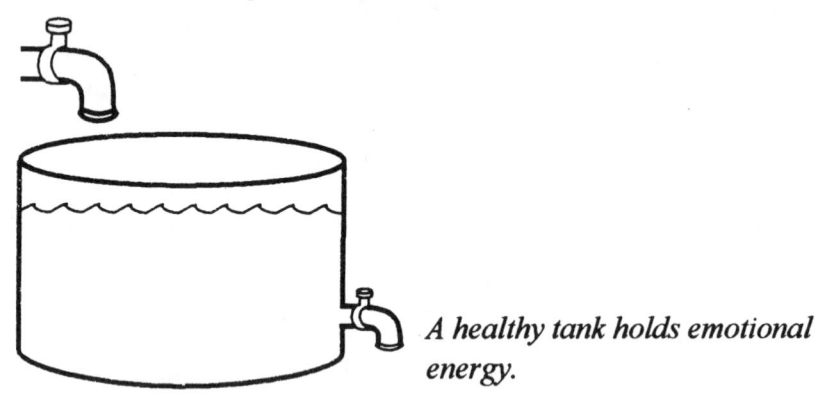

A healthy tank holds emotional energy.

It Takes the Love of Two Parents

You need both your parents in order to develop a healthy tank. You need the nurturing of a woman and of a man to develop your full potential as a person. If either of them was missing in your life, the sense of abandonment which follows will affect the development of your tank and your ability to exercise choices. Many of you learned to give up your choices because you didn't have what you needed from mom and dad.

A few of you grew up without your mothers. She may have left or been gone or been emotionally unavailable due to her own leaky tank. Ellen was seven years old when her baby sister, Alisha, was born. Her dad worked nights and slept through the day. He seldom made himself available for parenting either of his daughters. Ellen's mother felt overwhelmed with the new baby and in effect made Ellen her baby sister's mother. Ellen was the one who got up in the night when Alisha cried. When the baby was sick, Ellen stayed home from school. Ellen lost her childhood in her mother's attempt to avoid the pressures of motherhood. As an adult, Ellen still bears the wounds that early reversal of roles caused.

While *some* of you grew up without your mom, *most* of you grew up without your fathers. Your dad was gone to work or to play or to the bar. He may have abandoned the family altogether. You were raised by your mom or grandmother if there was a parent around at all. She was probably overwhelmed and overworked. She may have resented the fact that your father was gone, yet tried to teach the boys in the family that it was okay to be a male. Even if she tried her best not to dump her frustration with your father on you, she probably did so at least a little.

If you're a male and you grew up without your dad around, you have only a faint idea of what men are supposed to do and how they're supposed to think. You didn't have a guide to help you learn how to be a man. In other areas of your life, you learned by example. You learned to play a sport by playing and watching others play. You learned to work with your hands by building things yourself and by working with others who showed you how it was done. You learned to play, you learned to build, but there was no model to show you how to be a man. At best what you learned from watching your dad was to be gone, to be distant, to be critical and to be demanding. That's not adequate preparation for a choice-filled life.

What you missed most was having your dad be there for you. He was gone most of the time when you were growing up. He may have worked long hours at his job, or even worked two jobs, which kept him away from home sixty or more hours a week. Sundays were his day, so you would see little of him then. You remember few games of catch, infrequent and stressful family vacations, no help with homework, and very little sage, fatherly advice.

You can't learn to be a man without being around men. This is a simple and profound truth. Those of you who grew up without the presence of our fathers have a terrible time being male. You guess at what manhood is, often opting for stereotypes and caricatures instead of having any depth of personality.

If you're like most of middle class America, you spent most of your early years with your mother. Your mom did the best she could to give you a masculine side, but it was difficult to do when she herself felt the rejection of your dad's continuous absence. I've come to appreciate what a tough job it must have been for these women, isolated from the men in their lives and probably bitter about it, to teach us that it was acceptable to be a male.

If You Can't Say No You Can't Really Say Yes

For many or most of you, distance was your dad's MO. He had few close friends and it seemed to you that he could easily walk away from them if a place of tension came into their relationship. He treated his children the same way. He may have insured distance by being at work. Perhaps he was gone to the garage to work on one of the cars or one of his building projects.

Often the distance between fathers and their children was achieved through the television. There's a book about television called *The Plug In Drug*. That title certainly seems to describe the relationship between many fathers and their electronic eye on the world. Don't touch the channel. Don't talk too loudly while he's trying to watch. Don't walk between him and the picture. Dad, his TV, his VCR, his local TV listing and his remote control—a combination that's perfect for creating emotional distance.

Many of you could affirm that your father left you unprepared for life. Most of the things of any lasting importance you learned from your mom or your aunt or your grandmother. Few dads ever talked to their sons about sex, how to parent children, how to treat a woman, or what God is like.

Alan was sure that his father was the best dad he could be. He was convinced that his dad intended him no malice. He didn't mean to do him any harm. He wanted the best for his son and wanted him to have what he wanted out of life.

Having said that, Alan did believe that the way he was fathered left a gaping hole inside of him, a hole which he tried to fill with work, scholastic achievement, being good, looking good, being right, and being in control. He had asked his wife, his friends, and his children to fill that hole. Of course none of these people could heal the hole inside, but that didn't stop him from trying.

Because of his woundedness, Alan wounded others. It became imperative for him to admit his wounds if he was to live a quality life. Admitting his hurt and feeling his pain was the only thing that allowed him to reclaim his life.

Alan's dad never intended to hurt him. He didn't get up in the morning with a plan to injure his son. But he did hurt him. The result was a leaky tank and a damaged ability to make choices. If Alan is to have a quality life with a filled emotional reserve tank and power to choose, his tank has to be healed. And the only person who can do it is Alan.

The Pain of Outlandish Expectations

Jennifer's parents had tremendously high expectations of their children. They wanted them to be perfect and imagined that their offspring wanted the same thing. To that end, they would point out all their children's imperfections so they could correct them and dismiss these flaws. What they in fact did was create in their children a feeling of being one down, of never being good enough. It has taken Jennifer years of difficult work on her self-esteem and her perfectionism to even begin to accept the truth that she can be less than perfect and still be okay.

A man named Trevor remembered one story that illustrated how he felt rejected when he couldn't meet his father's expectations. It happened when he was 16. He remembered going with his dad to bring home some shelving. A friend of his dad's worked at a convenience store that was getting rid of its wooden shelving and replacing it with metal, adjustable shelving. As they attempted to push the shelving toward the door, it became obvious how heavy it was. Near the front of the store, Trevor and his father needed to lift the entire fixture in order to turn the corner and get it out the door. His father could lift his end, but Trevor couldn't budge his off the floor. Although he groaned and pushed, he couldn't make it past the turn.

Trevor had a cousin who had always been the athlete in the family. He was much smaller than Trevor, but very stocky and strong. When they were in the sixth grade they'd had a push-up contest. Trevor did 10. His cousin did 43. At this moment when Trevor and his dad were struggling to get that fixture out the door, when his desire to please was being overwhelmed by his physical limitations, his dad uttered words that hurt for years to come. "I wish your cousin was here," he said.

Nothing anyone ever said to him stung him more. The anguished reaction rattled around in his head. "Not good enough for you? I'm not good enough because I can't lift enough? I tell you what, I wish he were here, too. Then I wouldn't have to be!" Of course he said none of this out loud. But he was furious and hurt on the inside. He and his dad got that shelving out of the store, but he doesn't remember how. He only remembers the sting of that one sentence.

One of the most painful ways Margaret was injured was by being expected to be a mind reader when it can to deciphering what her mother wanted. She became a genius at attempting to anticipate what her mom wanted before she even asked. But no matter how hard she tried, she couldn't become perfect at the anticipation game.

When they would work together in the kitchen, Margaret was most often in charge of finding bowls and fetching the ingredients for her mother's culinary creations. She remembered being upset with herself if she couldn't see what her mom was going to need and have it in her hand when she asked for it. It wasn't even enough to be able to do this *some* of the time. Margaret expected perfection of herself. If she guessed wrong, she would put herself down inside. If her mother asked her to get something from the pantry, she would run so as not to delay her any more than was necessary.

The fact never occurred to Margaret that what she was trying to do was impossible. It wasn't until twenty years later that she began to realize the damage she'd done to herself by holding to such outrageous expectations.

Wounds: Abuse, Neglect, Rejection

Your tank can be damaged in a number of ways. Some of you were physically abused by your parents. The discipline you endured may have been severe. Some of you were beaten; there's no other word for it. Such abuse damages your tank.

Some of you were sexually abused by your mother, your father or another person in your life. You still carry within you the scars of that abusive behavior and the damage it has caused you. The adults who were supposed to nurture you used you instead. This damages your tank.

For many others, the wounds you feel weren't inflicted by physical or sexual abuse. What's missing for you was any sense of the positive in your life. You were put down, criticized and belittled. You were told you were no good or that you were flawed because you couldn't live up to your parent's expectations. Or maybe it was no communication of the positive things about you or your behavior. Nothing bad was said, but nothing was said at all. You weren't abused, you were neglected or abandoned. Without the loving care of an available parent, your tank will be damaged.

Much of the communication about not being good enough came in the form of sighs, looks of disgust, and noisy expressions of displeasure. Shoes left in the floor were kicked against the wall. Lights left on were turned off noisily by hitting the wall above the switch, followed by the brisk downward motion which made the bulb go dark. (For those of you who still nag and complain about lights left on, I recently checked with the local power company which told me that a 60-watt bulb uses 3.3 cents worth of electricity in 10 hours. This means that even if you leave six bulbs on all day, you still burn less than 20 cents worth of power—hardly enough to make much noise over!)

Most of what parents communicate they communicate nonverbally. That's just a fact of life. The bulk of what your parents communicated to you may have said, "What's wrong with you and don't you feel bad about that?" Those feelings of not being good enough have continued to follow you. They have been like cancer, eating up healthy tissue. It's impossible to have a healthy sense of yourself when you didn't measure up to the Giants who lived at the house with you when you were a child. The state of your tank reflects the results.

Healing Your Parental Wounds

The point of this discussion is self-inventory, not blame. It will do you no good to stay stuck in finger-pointing, pushing responsibility for your damaged tank onto your parents. While it's essential to acknowledge the actual condition of your tank, blaming your parents serves no purpose.

I once had a friend who went to therapy for two years, two times a week. At the end of that time I asked him, "What have you learned about yourself?"

My friend replied in a bitter tone, "I've learned that I hate my parents! They've really screwed me up!"

I asked him what he'd learned to do in response to such a strong emotion, but he had no answer. Two hundred therapy sessions and he hadn't begun the process of healing the love wounds that had been inflicted upon him by his mom and dad!

The point of this work isn't placing blame but promoting healing. The avenue to reach that end is grieving. If you didn't get what you needed, you'll feel hurt. Those wounds need to be healed. And healing starts when you allow yourself to feel the loss of what your younger self never received.

If your parents hurt you, they were probably suffering from the results of a low or damaged tank themselves. Their parents didn't nurture them either. The families that they grew up in didn't provide the setting they needed to develop healthy, filled, emotional reserve tanks.

One of the basic principles of tank building is this: If you don't have it, you can't give it away. Parents with damaged tanks can't raise sons and daughters who have healthy tanks. The path to effective parenting has to run through the ground of self-healing.

To whatever degree you haven't been loved by your parents, to that extent you won't be able to feel and give love. The situation is as simple and as complicated as that. You can't imagine anyone else accepting and loving you if you haven't received the love and acceptance of your parents. If the two people who co-created you couldn't love you, how could anyone else love you? "How," you'll ask yourself, "how can anyone love and accept me if my parents couldn't?" You'll push away others who offer you love. You'll feel too vulnerable to be close. You'll be sure he or she will leave you if he/she finds out how unlovable you feel, so you pretend that you feel more loved than you do. In order to carry on the charade, you have to keep distance between yourself and the other person. Your worst fear is that your friend or partner will get too close to you and discover the terrible truth you've attempted to hide.

Trevor and Alan, whose stories were described earlier in the chapter, are in their early 40s. They have moved away from home and been married to their wives for more than fifteen years. Still they've said that they long to hear their dads say, "You're a good kid. I love you!" As sons, they long to have dad's approval. It doesn't matter that a man is a father or even a grandfather himself. Without it he's like a ship that's built, but never commissioned. He stays in dry dock—full of promise but not using his full potential.

Just as Trevor and Alan wanted to hear an, "I love you" from their fathers, Margaret was dying inside, hoping that her mother would finally express her love to her. She continued to go out of her way to do things to receive mother's approval, even allowing her mom to invade her family and intrude on their routine, praying that finally her mother would show her the love she so wanted to see. But it never happened. For a long time she'd been meeting her mom's needs in the hope that her mother would eventually meet hers. One part of Margaret's healing was learning to let go of this unrealistic dream.

The Path to Healing

You have to do the hard work yourself. This work has many facets. Some of them are:
- Grieving wounds and losses
- Giving up addictions

- Reconnecting with your emotions
- Learning to reclaim and express your choices
- Growing spiritually

All of these challenging steps to healing will be described in the following chapters.

This is some of the hardest work you'll ever do, but the doing of it is essential to reclaiming your life and realizing the power of your choices. It takes tremendous courage to look, really look, at yourself and take steps to heal the woundedness you find there. If you're ready to do so, life can become richer in manifold ways.

The wounds you suffered at your parents' hands are real and require attention. Any unhealed hurts perpetuate the damage done to your tank and limit your ability to see and exercise choices. It's time to get busy. You're the only one who can do the work!

POWER TO CHOOSE: Complete the following sentence:
I am beginning to believe that. . .

_____

_____

_____

_____

_____

13

SOMETHING TERRIBLE HAPPENED!
Dealing With the Pain of Abuse

NATE WALKED INTO THE COUNSELING OFFICE with a confident, yet hesitant stride. His wife hadn't exactly sent him to therapy, but it was her complaints about his inability to allow himself to be close to her that had finally prompted him to come. He was genuinely concerned about his hesitancy to talk with his wife, to open up to her. He said he wanted things to change.

He was friendly and outgoing. On the outside, it looked as if nothing bothered him. However, on the inside, Nate knew things were much different. He was covering up the damage to his reserve tank and he knew it. He wanted to stop the pretense, but he wasn't sure he would have the courage to do so. He hoped that this time he'd be able to take the risk to share his secret. Nate wanted to reveal what he'd been working so long and hard to conceal: he'd been sexually abused as a child. That sexual abuse had damaged his tank.

A tank is damaged by abuse.

If you knew him, you probably wouldn't have guessed his secret. He'd been through the common rowdy stage in high school, including a time of experimentation with alcohol and drugs, but you'd have had to look closely to see that this was a way to deal with his pain. He joined the military right out of high school, where the rigid routine and continuing use of alcohol and drugs allowed him to cope with his secret. As he completed his time in the military, he stopped abusing alcohol and drugs and met and married the girl of his dreams. In the five years of their marriage, he threw himself into his work. It was common for him to be on the job 65 to 70 hours a week. He was always outgoing and friendly. He was faithful in his church attendance, even teaching a class. Still, he didn't feel good about his life.

Shutting Down the System

One of the reasons Nate felt so empty was that he'd shut down his emotional system. In order to protect himself from the painful and shameful memory of his abuse, he'd numbed himself out. First using alcohol and drugs and now using work, he was able to stay out of touch with his emotions. While this strategy for coping with his pain was effective in keeping Nate distanced from his feelings, it was emptying his tank and robbing him of choices.

Your emotional reserve tank has an electrical system that's much like the one that protects your house. In your home there are a series of circuit breakers which provide safety in the case of an electrical short. Using these circuit breakers, it's possible to turn off any light fixture, base plug or appliance in the house using one of the individual circuit breaker switches. There's also one main breaker that will turn off the power to the entire house.

There are two ways that these breakers can be turned off. First, you could turn one or more of them off intentionally, as would be the safe practice before working on a light fixture or base plug. The other way the electrical power could get switched off would be when one of the breakers blows due to an electrical short. A light bulb or appliance that shorted out could cause the breaker to trip, interrupting power to that part of the house.

While it's possible to turn off every light and plug in the house using this system, it's not possible to turn off just one. Several are on each breaker, which means that when power to one is stopped, power to several more is also interrupted. If four plugs in a room are on the same circuit, you can't turn off the breaker and still use one of the plugs. The power to them all is shut down.

Whether a breaker is turned off or is tripped because of some problem, power won't be restored automatically. A conscious effort must be made to turn the switch back on before the circuit will again be fully functional. If the power is restored and a problem still exists in the system, the breaker will trip again. In such a case, you'll have to search for the source of the continuing problem if the system is to function properly.

This circuit breaker system isn't designed to cause frustration, although it may be frustrating if a problem persists that causes the breakers to blow repeatedly. The purpose of the system is to protect the appliances and other electrical gadgets, the structure itself, and those who live within it.

The wiring of your reserve tank parallels this electrical system. When something traumatic occurs in your life, a part of you can shut down. You may be afraid that you'll be unable to meet the challenge being presented, so your system interrupts power. Your emotional system can be shut down when you've been abused, experienced some other kind of trauma, or when someone close to you dies. This interruption in your emotional power can allow you to get through the emotional challenge.

Interruptions to your reserve tank's electrical system can take one of four forms:

- Minimizing—"What happened really wasn't that bad."
- Rationalizing—"What happened was bad, but you can't blame him because..."
- Forgetting—The memory of the events is turned off.
- Denying—"Of course I remember, but I'll never admit that to you!"

Nate's system shut down when he was abused. At the age of eleven when the abuse occurred, he didn't have the resources to deal with what happened. His system shut down as he minimized and rationalized his pain so he could go on with his life. However, dealing with trauma by shutting down takes a tremendous toll on the level in the reserve tank. There came a point when he realized that he wasn't living, he was just existing. He wanted more out of life. He wanted to experience all of life.

It's necessary to reestablish power so that full emotional function can be restored. If this doesn't happen, a part of you remains inactive. You'll also make choices based on your desire to stay insulated from your painful feelings, thus negatively influencing your ability to make choices. Your ability to choose will be hindered. Nate needed to face his abuse in order to reclaim his choices.

Getting Back in Touch

Heather had never grieved the death of her mother. She'd died nine years before she first came to see her counselor. She initially sought counseling because her marriage was breaking up. As she continued her counseling relationship, she was able to see how the death of her mother and her marriage problems were related.

Her family had never talked about what it was like to lose their wife and mother. Dad had quickly remarried and Heather felt it would be painful to her step-mother to talk about the death of her mom and dad's first wife. Besides, the family had a history of superficial communication before mom ever died. Not only had she not talked to her family, she'd never talked to a friend or to her husband about mom's death. Heather hadn't allowed herself to grieve her mother's death, so she'd shut down the emotional side related to her passing. This emotional numbing out inhibited her ability to be emotionally involved with her husband.

The way she'd handled her mother's death also affected Heather's willingness to trust. She remembered thinking, "I'll never let anyone get this close to me again!" as she pushed aside the pain of her mother's death. That vow of distance from others included her spouse, although she wasn't conscious of it at the time. For the five years they'd been married, she'd worked to keep him at a distance. She did this through the long hours of overtime in her work schedule, by not talking about anything of any real consequence when she came home, and by staying busy around the house when she was home. Her choice to keep such a distance between herself and her husband wasn't premeditated, although the damage done to her marriage would have been the same if she'd done it intentionally.

Heather began the process of turning her circuit breakers back on when she allowed herself to grieve her mother's death. Experiencing the loss of her mom was almost overwhelming at times, but it allowed her to feel again and to trust again. She came to see that being born, living and dying are all part of a cycle of life that can't be altered. When she began the process of accepting her mother's death, she was able to allow herself to be closer to the folks around her. The only way she could regain her personal power and refill her tank was to allow herself to admit the pain of her mother's death and grieve this great loss.

Forgetting as a Way of Coping

Your ability to forget can protect you from the painful memory of a wound you were unable to deal with at the time. When the hurtful events occur, you can interrupt the part of yourself that even remembers what happened. The result is a coping mechanism that's often very effective, but which once again leaves part of your life outside your control. Reserve tank energy is lost and personal power is limited.

I have seen this repeatedly with victims of traumatic events, such as accidents, tragic loss, and physical, emotional and sexual abuse. It's been fascinating to me to watch what happens when the circuit is turned back on and memory returns. This can often be a painful time, but a time which can afford great personal growth. Working through the pain heals the weak places in the tank and increases the level in the reserve tank.

With work your tank can be healed.

Janet was 25 years old before she was ready to remember and deal with her sexual abuse. Her abuser was her older brother, who was often left in charge of baby-sitting her while their parents were at work. While they were alone together, her brother had often coerced her into performing oral sex on him. The abuse began when she was seven and continued for three years, ceasing when her brother graduated from high school and moved out of the house.

At the age of seven, Janet wasn't emotionally equipped to deal with what had happened. She was afraid that no one would believe her if she told. She didn't know what was really happening, but she knew it didn't feel right.

Her way of coping with her abuse was to shut down part of herself. She forgot what had happened: completely, utterly, convincingly. For nearly fifteen years she didn't recall what had occurred.

One day the power was reinstated. It happened unexpectedly while she was watching a television program about women who'd been sexually abused. When one of the young women on the program mentioned that she'd completely forgotten the episodes of abuse for many years, Janet realized that this was what she'd done. As the program continued, she was overwhelmed with the memory of what had happened to her so many years ago.

Forgetting had served a very important purpose for Janet. It had enabled her to get through the next several years. At the age of nine, she wasn't equipped to understand completely nor to resolve adequately what had happened to her. Without the ability to turn off this part of herself, she might have been overwhelmed by what her brother had done.

After she'd watched that television program, she realized that forgetting would no longer work for her. It takes a tremendous amount of energy to forget. Eventually, remembering is essential to having a full life.

Choosing to Grieve

Unresolved wounds take a tremendous toll on your emotional reserve tank. First, they damage the tank, leaving holes in the tank itself. Energy which is added to the tank runs out and is lost. Like a bucket with a hole in it, the contents of the tank are spilled. The damage to the walls of the tank has to be repaired.

Further, the level in the tank isn't as high as it should be because some fillers are missed. The hurt and lack of trust lead you to distance yourself from other people, missing out on the healthy connection with others which could fill your tank. Trust is an issue, causing you to look at others with suspicion. Passion in your life may be missing because you spend so much of your time and energy holding back. You don't have the freedom to be yourself. Many potential fillers are unavailable until the loss is resolved.

Damaged tank: missed fillers and unexpressed grief.

Finally, the tank is emptied due to the emotional cost of forgetting or the depletion caused by harbored anger, unexpressed grief and loss of self-esteem. Anger unexpressed doesn't dissipate. It stays with you, exacting tremendous levels of energy from your reserve. Your self-esteem also suffers when you haven't resolved the pain of being hurt and abused because you see yourself as less than others. Until you're willing to admit the hurt, it's common to constantly measure yourself by others and come up short.

The good news is that adults can choose. You can choose to remember. Grownups can struggle through the unfinished business of past traumas. You can make a choice to explore the dark places inside of yourself. You can choose to begin the healing.

Healing: Tough, but Worth It

It's difficult to admit that you've been sexually abused. The sense of victimization and the shame with which you may come to view yourself make it hard to accept the fact that you were taken advantage of by someone else. Difficult memories will have to be recalled. Painful emotions will need to be felt.

There are often questions that you'll want answered, questions that don't have easy answers:

"Why did this happen to *me*?"

"Where were my parents? Why didn't they *protect* me?"

"Where was God? Why wasn't he taking care of me?"

There's an additional complication for males who have been sexually abused. Since most perpetrators are males, males are most often abused by other males. Being abused by a same-sex perpetrator adds the stigma of homosexuality to the list of issues to be confronted. You may wonder if you're a homosexual, especially if you found yourself aroused by the situation. Of course, this fear makes admission and/or disclosure more difficult.

The truth is that there's an automatic, physiological response to sexual stimulation. Whatever the source, your body may respond with arousal. If this happened to you during your abuse, it has nothing to do with homosexual tendencies or desires. It just means that the wiring in your body was functioning and responsive to the sensations.

The process of remembering is often difficult. Janet, the woman you read about earlier in this chapter, had an extremely trying time when it came to talking about how she'd been sexually abused by her brother. In counseling, she reached an impasse when it came to remembering and releasing what had happened. She'd been able to talk about her abuse in general terms, but had been unable to remember and release the details.

During one of her sessions, the therapist she was working with tried something new. Using a family of anatomically correct dolls to help her reveal the story, Janet was able to act out what happened. She felt a little uncomfortable at first—a twenty-five year old playing with dolls in order to tell her story—but she was able to tell what happened using these props. At each step along the way, Janet would say to herself, "I can do this! I can do this!" She in fact was able to tell her story, an important step in the healing process.

Resources for Healing

If you've remembered or you suspect you've been abused, or if you have another kind of trauma or loss to resolve, there are some practical steps you can take. Remember that healing is important. Only when the pain is resolved will you regain your personal power to choose.

When you're ready to deal with the shutdowns in your emotional system, what can you do? These suggestions can help. As always, use these gently and carefully.

- Before you leave your way of coping, celebrate your coping mechanism. Recognize the ways in which it served you. It's extremely important to honor your resourcefulness in coping with your past in this way before moving on.
- Schedule time for contemplating and remembering. Years may have been spent in minimizing, rationalizing, forgetting and denying. It may be necessary to prime the pump if you're to restore your system to full functioning. A certain time of the day or week can be designated as your time to remember. Start

with short sessions of ten or twenty minutes, then increase the length of time as it's best for you.
- Write about what you're dealing with. Writing assists you in defining reality. Writing serves as a catharsis to help you empty "it" out on paper. ("It" is whatever happened to you.) Writing can be an important part of the grieving process. In addition, your pen and paper can be there when people can't be. (Go slowly with this suggestion because writing make things very *real*.)
- As you choose to remember, you can also choose the rate at which you remember. If things become too intense, you can slow down or stop. Give yourself time. Come back to the issues, but do it on your own schedule. If you're making good progress, add to the amount of time you're spending if that would be helpful.
- You'll need to be talking to someone about what has happened. Keeping your pain, trauma or abuse a secret can increase your sense of shame. Not telling implies that what has happened is untellable. Choose a listener carefully. You'll want someone who'll listen, but won't judge, reject or attempt to fix you.
- Many books have been written on this subject which may be helpful for you. Check with your local library or bookstore for a list of possible resources.
- If you aren't making the kind of progress you want to experience, you may want to enlist the help of a professional. Many counselors and therapists have been trained to deal with the issues which result from trauma and abuse.

Remember that you can do this healing work without ever talking to the persons who abused you. One of the first questions Janet asked was, "Will I have to talk to my brother?" It was obvious from the tone of her inquiry that she didn't want to do so. I assured her that whether or not she ever confronted her abuser was entirely her choice. She didn't have to talk to him in order to get well. What was important was to clean out the garbage inside so that she was no longer ruled by her history.

The process of healing can be a long and difficult process. It can take months, even years to heal the damage done to the reserve tank. In addition, the process of forgiving is a necessary, yet challenging step toward regaining your choices. You'll learn more about forgiveness in the next chapter.

Be patient. The work is worth it.

If You Can't Say No You Can't Really Say Yes

POWER TO CHOOSE: When have you used the following to deal with your past?

Minimizing

_____
_____
_____
_____

Rationalizing

_____
_____
_____
_____

Forgetting

_____
_____
_____
_____

Denying

_____
_____
_____
_____

14

HOARDING WORTHLESS STONES
Understanding Forgiveness

NOTHING IS MORE of a threat to your ability to make choices than unforgiven hurts. The energy that's required to maintain the memory of wrongs which you haven't yet forgiven can leave you feeling empty and tired. The anger and resentment of holding onto past pain is a slow, but very steady, drain on your emotional reserve tank.

Your tank is depleted by unforgiven hurts.

As important as forgiving is, it often doesn't occur. You may have been too stubborn to let "bygones be bygones." At other times, you may not have known you needed to forgive. Some of you have even thought that you shouldn't forgive another person because he or she hadn't yet asked for forgiveness or because you didn't want to let the other person off the hook.

Suppose you've decided you want to forgive a person, but you don't know how to do so. Is it possible to forgive your parents for the hurts they've inflicted? Can you forgive a spouse or partner who had an affair? How is it possible to pardon a betrayed confidence? Can the unkind words spoken by your spouse in the heat of arguments for years and years be forgiven?

The answer is a resounding, "Yes!" In fact, it's not only possible, it's imperative.

When someone hurts you, the wrong they have done separates you. The hurt can't be brushed aside. The presence of this pain interrupts closeness, drains your reserve tank and limits your choices. The reserve tank is drained by the cost of maintaining the resentment, hurt and anger you experience. Your choices are limited because of your clouded judgment and your perceived loss of options. When you haven't forgiven, you often *react* rather than *act*, cutting off many of the possible choices you could have made.

If you're to maximize your personal power to choose, forgiveness is a *must*, not an option. Bruised feelings will have to be healed. Trust must be rebuilt. The hurts which have been inflicted will have to be carefully addressed.

Since you're imperfect, live in an imperfect world and have relationships with other people who are imperfect, forgiveness is essential. You can't live a choice-filled life without it.

A Common Question

Before getting into the process of forgiveness, there's one misconception that it's important to address. This question has to do with the meaning of the phrase, "Forgive and forget." I often hear a comment that goes something like this when it comes to forgiving a tough hurt: "Well I *may* be able to forgive him/her, but I can *never* forget!" Usually the meaning of this sentence isn't as vicious as it sounds. Often what I find is that the person with the concern is truly struggling with what it means to forget.

It's sometimes imagined that forgetting implies being able to erase completely from your memory the fact that a hurt occurred. In the middle of the pain you experience in dealing with an undeserved hurt, it's impossible to imagine that this could ever happen.

The truth is that it's not possible to choose to lose your memory with respect to the thing you've forgiven. To forget doesn't mean that you've gotten amnesia. It simply means that you choose no longer to hold the hurt against the other person.

Forgiveness implies a letting go. Something is released which separates people. When forgiveness occurs, walls are broken down and full relationship is once again possible. But you don't have to have your brain erased with respect to what happened. Brain surgery isn't called for; amnesia simply isn't necessary.

The Process of Forgiving

Let's use an illustration to describe the process of forgiveness. Suppose you've finished a shopping spree at the mall. As you leave the shopping center, you're standing on the curb outside the stores ready to cross the street to your car. As you wait with your packages in hand, a car driving by begins to weave back and forth across the road, clearly out of control. The car runs up on the curb, runs over your foot, knocks you down, and sends your packages flying.

The driver finally wrestles the car to a stop 20 feet past you. As it turns out, he's someone you know, a close friend. He comes running back to you, asking how you are and apologizing profusely. He tells you that the steering on the car simply wouldn't respond to his direction. The car careened out of control, failing to react to anything he did.

Here's the question: Even though you now know *why* the car ran over your foot and you know that the driver didn't intend you any harm, are you still in pain? Does your foot still hurt? Does the fact that you've heard an explanation take away your injury? Does the desire to keep a friendship negate the wound you have sustained? Will the simple longing to put this behind you be enough to move you toward healing? The answer to all these questions is, of course, no.

If you've been injured, you have choices as to how you'll handle your pain. You could *deny* it. You could "walk it off" like football coaches sometimes tell their players to do after an especially hard hit in a game. If you've been hurt significantly, you may even limp, but if you're into denial, you try to deny even the limp.

You could *minimize* your injury by saying it's not significant. "It's no big deal," you might insist. "I can handle this," you could affirm. Meanwhile, bones may be protruding from your foot and blood may be oozing from a cut.

You could *rationalize* your pain. "He didn't mean to hurt me. Although I'm hurt, it wasn't intentional. I shouldn't complain. I'm sure he did the best he could."

If you want to start the healing process, you must begin by *admitting your hurt.* This is the only way forgiveness can begin. Then you must *feel your pain.* This means saying, "Ouch!" as loudly and as long as you need to in order to express how wounded you are. Next you must face the challenge of *healing.* At the very least that means giving yourself time to mend. It may mean seeking help or going for treatment. If your foot is severely injured, healing may necessitate days or weeks of recuperation. You may need to put your foot up and rest. Finally, there's the challenge to *restore the relationship.* Can the two of you once again be reconciled so that your relationship is maintained?

This entire process is motivated by love and is fueled by a desire to release the other person and yourself from the bondage of unforgivingness. And it's the only way to restore your power to choose. If you won't forgive, then your sense of personal power will be limited.

Admit your hurt. Feel your pain. Seek healing within yourself. Restore the relationship. These four parts of the process of forgiveness will occur in a repeated cycle as you move from admitting your hurt to feeling your pain and on to healing only to discover that there's more hurt to admit. Given time to focus on what needs to be forgiven, and having the desire to put it behind you, forgiveness can occur using this four-step model.

Admit Your Hurt

Hurts can take a multitude of forms. Consider these examples of hurts received in differing kinds of relationships:

- You've been chastised by your boss, again, in front of your co-workers.
- A confidence you shared with a trusted friend comes back to you.
- A parent who was supposed to love and nurture you as a child, abused you instead.
- A husband injures his wife's self-esteem with criticism or put downs.
- A wife inflicts pain on her husband during her monthly bouts with PMS. She knows she's out of control each month for four or five days, but she hasn't found a way to cease the attacks.
- You learn that your spouse is having an affair.

The pain of these and scores of other issues and situations calls for attention. Whether the wound inflicted involves actual malice, betrayal, or being ignored, there's a common thread running through all of these forms of hurt: you were unfairly treated. You deserved better, but received worse. You were hurt and the pain calls for attention. When you hurt so badly, how is forgiveness possible?

The first step in the process is simply this: choosing to admit the reality of the pain you've suffered. No pretending is allowed. You have to admit that something has happened which has hurt you. You can't talk tough or stay stuck in a macho routine.

Remember that ignoring or remaining out of touch with a feeling doesn't make it go away. Emotions are energy and emotions which are unexpressed are stored energy. The force of these stuffed feelings can cause messy explosions. Hurts which haven't been admitted limit your power to choose as you dump on, withdraw from and perhaps abuse others.

Focusing on how you've been hurt isn't the same as living in the past or picking your own wounds. You have to be honest with the pain you've experienced. This is the first step to finding the care you need. A doctor who's attempting to treat a patient wants first to know the extent of his wounds. Where are you hurt? How badly? What are your vital signs? Only when the actual condition of his patient is known can the physician assist in the healing process with the maximum chance for success.

Feel Your Pain

Anger. Rejection. Betrayal. Hurt. Hatred. These are but a few of the emotional responses you may have to the injury another person has inflicted on you. The challenge at this point is to feel the pain. You have to say, "Ouch!" as loudly as the pain that has been inflicted would dictate. Then the process of regaining your choices can begin.

Your response may be anger. Anger is a signal that one of your boundaries has been violated. It's a sign that something has been done which transgresses a value which you hold. Anger demands attention.

Your pain may take the form of hatred. Hatred has been described as a snarling tiger in the soul. It's ravenous, devouring you and other people around you. Hate is wishing your former spouse would get a sexually transmitted disease from sexual exploits. It's a sense that justice isn't being done and that you're the one who's paying the price.

Perhaps you've heard the story of a man who answered an ad for a new Volvo. The total asking price was $250. The man, thinking that the price must be a misprint, drove to the address listed in the ad. The woman of the house assured him the price was correct. He thought, "Something terrible must be wrong with the car." To his surprise he found that the car was in mint condition. No dents or scrapes. And it ran like a dream. "Perhaps it's stolen," he thought. No, she had a clear title. He paid the woman who placed the ad $250 and drove away in his new car.

Before he could even get home, guilt overwhelmed him. He returned to the woman's house. "Lady, this car is worth thousands. I feel as if I have taken advantage of you. I can't leave like this until I know why you're selling this car at such a low price."

The woman asked him to wait, went into the next room and returned with a telegram. "My husband left me a month ago," she said. "He and his secretary have been in Jamaica since then. Two days ago I received this telegram from him." The telegram read in part, "AM RUNNING SHORT ON MONEY. STOP. SELL VOLVO. STOP. SEND PROCEEDS." This woman had been severely hurt and was feeling her hatred. She would sell the car, but at a price that would inflict pain on her wayward husband.

Hatred can take two general forms, active and passive. Active hatred causes you to strike out. Like the woman in this story, you do something to express how you feel. Hatred can also take a passive form. You don't act, but you don't wish the other person well either. You may feel a small smile when he suffers misfortune himself. Regardless of the form it takes, your hatred limits your power. When you live in hatred, you allow yourself to be another person's prisoner.

Some people are surprised to learn that love and hate can both be strongly felt for the same person. A man may love his wife for her devotion to the children but hate her for her thoughtless indifference to his needs. A woman can love her husband, but hate him on a particular day because he's been insensitive.

Hatred doesn't contribute to fulfilled living. It's presence is a negative force that drains energy from your tank. Hate is like a cancer that eats at you. Chronic hatred is one of the biggest depleters for your reserve tank. If your goal is to regain your power to choose, hatred must eventually be released.

Your pain may be in the form of rejection. Your friend may act differently when others are around. When you're alone together, she may seem pleased to be with you. However, when certain others are around, she may seem embarrassed to be around you. That rejection hurts.

It's important to stay with your feelings so that you can identify the emotion you're actually feeling. If you feel betrayed or rejected, but believe it would be inappropriate to feel those emotions, your pain may be expressed as anger. While you may vent your frustration through anger, if you're actually feeling another emotion, you'll get stuck in the process of healing.

Wishing your pain wasn't present or pretending it isn't there won't take it away. The process of forgiving demands that you face the pain. You admit your feelings. When you embrace them instead of stuffing them, you can begin to let go. Letting go will often be a slow process. The hurts may run deep. They may have occurred numerous times. But if forgiveness is to be real, you'll have to admit, name and feel your pain.

Many people have found that writing helps them be honest about how they feel. Writing serves several useful purposes. First, it's a way to empty out what's inside. Writing can be a catharsis which releases you from the pain held within. Second, writing can provide answers. A path through the struggle may become apparent when the feelings and memories are externalized. Third, a person can write when no one is around to talk to. If a woman is struggling with her history of sexual abuse as a teenager and wakes from a dream about the perpetrator at two in the morning, calling a friend to talk about the pain may not be prudent. Writing can help.

Seek Healing Within Yourself

The healing process takes place inside of you. No one else can do it for you. You can't ask your spouse to take care of this task. Healing can't come from the outside. It's only possible to close old wounds when you allow healing energy to flow from within you toward the person who has hurt you.

This phase in the cycle comes to life as you adopt a new way of looking at the ones who have hurt you. You come to see how weak and needy they are. It was out of their imperfection that they have inflicted their own pain upon you. In the process of healing, you come to see that the person who hurt you is separate from the hurt he or she inflicted on you. Only then are you able to forgive.

If you attempt to heal yourself too early in the forgiveness process, you'll only minimize your pain instead of healing your heart. If you try to skip the first two parts of the process, failing to admit your hurt and feel your pain, you'll tend to rationalize the destructive actions of the other person. Early on in the process, statements like, "I know she has her own problems," or, "He did the best he could" can easily be ways to make light of your pain.

Marie and Philip have been married for ten years. To hear them talk, these have been ten very *long* years. When they married, Marie brought two young children to the relationship. Philip had never parented children before, so he was new to the world of bedtime stories, spilled milk, temper tantrums and childish forgetfulness. His way of coping with any problems with the kids was to demand, argue and yell. Sometimes he yelled at the children and sometimes he yelled at Marie. By the time they came to counseling, she said she wasn't sure she wanted the marriage to go on.

Marie said she was tired of the noise even though Philip had made a remarkable change about two years before they came to therapy. He'd stopped yelling, attempting instead to express his desires for the children in quiet tones backed up by consequences that didn't involve increasing levels of volume. He'd begun to woo his wife, bringing home flowers and notes and making telephone calls to her in the middle of the day for no reason. Both Marie and Philip said that he'd been very consistent in maintaining his new behavior. But Marie had a problem. After all the years of screaming and verbal attacks, she said that she couldn't forgive Philip. Whenever they talked about their marriage, she always recounted his many sins which had occurred during their first eight years of marriage.

At their first session, the therapist began by having each of them make a resentment list. This was to be a complete and extensive list of all the wrongs each one believed he or she had suffered at the hands of the other. The point behind the assignment was two-fold. First, by listing all the wrongs they'd suffered, they could experience a catharsis as they emptied these out. Second, as the spouses read their lists in the session, each would be sure that the other had heard his or her pain.

After several sessions, Marie continued to hang on to her pain. She continued to bring up events and issues that had happened years ago in the early stages of their marriage. The counselor finally asked her a difficult question. "Can you find it in your heart to forgive your husband?" Her first response was an emphatic, "No!" But as she thought about the possibility of any future together, she came to realize that the only way to have any kind of life with Philip was to forgive him. She also came to realize that she, too, needed forgiveness from Philip. After careful thought, she decided to take the risk of letting go.

This next part may sound corny or too easy to you, but the only force that's powerful enough to enable you to forgive is the power of love. You learn to despise the hurt, but love the hurter. It may sound too simple or simplistic, but it's not easy. If you aren't able to make this distinction between the person and what he or she did, you'll remain stuck in unforgivingness. Your tank will be depleted. Your power to choose will be limited. The only way to get loose from the past and regain your power to choose is to forgive.

An important part of the healing process is the renewal of trust. When a hurt has occurred, violations of trust have occurred. Sometimes these violations have been monstrous in size. Trust will need to be renewed if a relationship is to continue.

These violations of trust can take two basic forms: active or passive. Active violations would include such things as having an affair, telling lies, spending money in damaging ways, or saying things to hurt the other person. Passive forms would include not meeting the legitimate needs a person has for conversation, touch and sexual expression, constant withdrawal from your partner, or being unresponsive to the requests of your spouse. Whether trust was lost due to active or passive means is in many ways immaterial. Both hurt. The distinction is made here to help you look for the origin of your pain.

If your relationship is to improve, trust must be rebuilt. It takes time and consistency of behavior to accomplish this. You'll have to go slowly and allow time for the process to happen.

I once worked with a couple who had failed to recognize the need to move on to the refreshing healing of forgiveness. These parents had found out that their teenage daughter had been sleeping with her boyfriend. In a session the wife mentioned that she'd forgiven her daughter because she'd asked for forgiveness. I asked if she'd forgiven the young man. In a bitter voice she informed me that not only had she *not* forgiven him, but that she thought it would be wrong for her to do so since the young man had not *asked* for forgiveness. Her husband seconded this view of forgiveness. Their misunderstanding of the process of forgiveness made both of them prisoners to their bitter feelings, feelings which interrupted their ability to love and to enjoy life. These feelings significantly hindered their power to choose, resulting in an extremely low level in their reserve tanks.

Restoring the Relationship

When someone hurts you, the wrong they've done separates you. That wrong is so significant that it can't be easily brushed aside. Acknowledging the hurt and feeling the pain is the beginning of the process of coming back together. Healing yourself is a vital part of the process as you see them as people, warts and all, and *choose* to forgive. The final step is reaching out to them to restore the relationship.

Restoration of the relationship can only happen when you begin to let the past be the past. You have to be willing to let go and move on.

This process of restoration requires something of the other person. It means that he or she must attempt to feel what you felt. Reconciliation is possible only if that person is able to grieve the hurt he or she caused you. The other person must be willing to listen, to clearly hear your pain, even if it takes many repetitions of the story. And there must be a promise. This promise concerns the present and future that you and the other person have with one another. The promise is that the person who hurt you will promise never to hurt you that way again. Such a promise is often difficult to keep perfectly, but keeping it must be the intent.

You'll frustrate yourself and others if you seek to reconcile without facing your hurt. In the same way, you'll be thwarted if you seek to be reconciled with anyone who hurt you if he or she hasn't made this pledge not to inflict further pain. I have worked with a number of people who were intent on getting their relationship back together no matter what the cost. They never heard the other person say, "I'm sorry. As far as it is within my power, I'll never hurt you again in this way." Still they go ahead with their efforts to put the relationship back together. In the process they often set themselves up to be hurt again.

The Process Works

This model for achieving forgiveness will work if you'll work it. It's not easy. It's certainly not painless. But it does work.

Alex and Sarah were a couple who had drifted apart over time. Their work schedules had left little time for being together. He was a busy lawyer and she was in management for a large corporation. Sarah felt unwanted and unloved by her husband and sought affirmation outside the marriage. She found it with another man. At first they just talked. Over time the relationship became increasingly physical. Their sexual relationship had been continuing for several months when Alex discovered it.

His first response was to file for divorce. He did so that very afternoon. However, as they began to talk things through, they both decided that they didn't want to divorce. They wanted to make right what had gone wrong in the marriage. There was one very big obstacle: How could they forgive one another?

They worked through the steps in this cycle of forgiveness. There were long talks and lots of questions as they admitted their hurt and expressed their pain. They worked through the step of personal healing. Two times they were so overwhelmed with the size of the job that they almost gave up.

Finally they moved to the point of restoring the relationship. They were more solid as a couple than they'd ever been. With a promise to one another not to hurt one another in such a way again, they recommitted themselves to one another.

Not all stories turn out with this sort of happy ending, but many can. It's difficult work, but forgiveness is definitely possible.

POWER TO CHOOSE: The most difficult aspect of forgiveness for me is . . .

_____
_____
_____
_____
_____

One more question: What do you want to do about it?

_____
_____
_____
_____
_____

PART FOUR

Facing Special Challenges

15

SEX IS MORE THAN BODY PARTS
Developing a Healthy Sexuality

HARRY AND ELAINE HAD COMPLAINTS about their sex life. When sex, which Harry defined as intercourse, occurred, it was good. Both enjoyed it. The frequency was the problem. Harry wanted sex much more often than did his wife. Elaine didn't necessarily want it more often, but she did want to feel closer to her husband and she knew that a more frequent sex life would contribute to this.

Harry's way of encouraging Elaine to be sexual more often was to complain, mope, pout and have long talks until two in the morning about the problems with their sex life. Sometimes he put her down in anger and frustration. Of course, Harry's put downs and complaints aimed at Elaine had an affect which was exactly the opposite of the one he wanted. She withdrew from him and was becoming less and less interested in their sexual relationship.

The solution Harry had chosen to deal with the problem wasn't working. He needed to see how his solution was adversely affecting his wife, so I told him a story.

"Imagine that you come upon this scene," I began. "You see a man standing beside his car at the side of a busy highway. You pull off to see if you can help. You find him kicking his car and yelling at the top of his lungs, calling the car all kinds of names. As you walk up to him, you ask him what's wrong. He tells you the car is out of gas.

"Out of gas? That's not the car's fault, is it? When cars are out of gas, no amount of yelling, blaming, complaining or pleading will change the situation. The only way to change the situation is to take the steps necessary to put gas into the tank!

"Harry, your sexual relationship with Elaine is like that car. She is running out of gas. Pressuring her to perform won't help. Your response is making matters worse. Your anger only empties her tank further. What you have to do is find out what fills her tank, then work with her to fill it up. Are you willing to listen to what she has to say? Would you be willing to work with her so that the level in her tank can rise and she'll be in a position to say yes more often?" When Harry heard his wife's plight described in this way, he said he'd be willing to work harder at being a tank-filler than he'd been up to that point.

This couple was fortunate in that they sought help before there were pushed apart by years of resentment. They had no other major problems and were both willing to focus on changing their way of dealing with this issue. By concentrating on what was necessary to fill the tank, they were able to move toward the increased intimacy they desired.

Sex Is In How You See It

Most of what happens in a couple's sexual relationship is a result of the way they think about sex and the level of sharing or intimacy they're experiencing. There's more to sex than glands, gonads, sweat and panting. Yet all too often this is the focus of sexual expression in our culture. The truth is that the length or depth of the genitals, the size of chests, breasts or buttocks, or the turn of the legs has little to do with the pleasure a couple finds in their sexual expression. Some of my best looking clients have had the poorest sex lives.

Sex is an extension of a couple's emotional relationship. It's a physical testimony to the amount of emotional closeness they share. When there is little intimacy, sex will be infrequent and/or dissatisfying. There's little to express, so little is expressed physically.

Too many men have learned about their sexuality from television, movies and the media. In order to hold the viewer's attention, actors and directors must dramatize their subject. When they do this with sex and a man buys into the production, he sets himself up to be frustrated. James Bond may fuel your fantasies of sexual expression with a woman, but it's not reality and it won't work in your bedroom.

Women have also been sold a false view of sexuality. Movies with happily ever after endings aren't reality. Harlequin novels paint an unattainable picture of emotional satisfaction and physical attraction. In real life prostitutes seldom wind up with rich businessmen, living happily ever after, the plot for the widely-viewed movie "Pretty Woman." Real life couples have ups and downs, good days and bad. They'll look more like the characters played by Debra Winger and Billy Crystal in "Forget Paris."

Sex and the Reserve Tank

Let's return to the reserve tank introduced in Chapter 3. Remember that the tank looks like this:

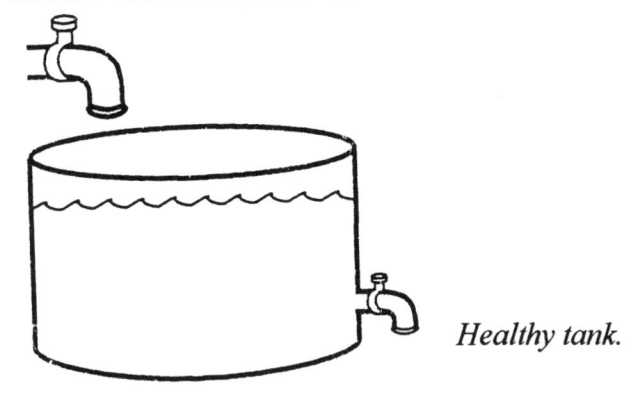

Healthy tank.

From my work with couples, it seems clear that the outlet for sexual expression is higher up on the tank, so that a fairly full tank is necessary before sexual sharing can be fulfilling. There has to be an adequate reserve in the tank if sexual expression is to be satisfying to both partners. The sexual outlet is affixed to the tank like this:

Relatively full tank necessary for satisfying sexual expression.

The level in the tank has to be relatively high in order for there to be a spontaneous expression of sexuality. When the reserve is low, there's no flow into the line leading to sexual expression. The only way to get any energy to flow out of the tank is to tilt the tank.

Tilting the tank may make it possible temporarily for emotional energy to flow through the sexual outlet, but doing so will raise anxiety about how much energy there will be left to meet other requirements of daily living once the sexual encounter is over and the wife or husband places the tank back in it's upright position.

If You Can't Say No You Can't Really Say Yes

Tilting the tank: a temporary solution at best.

Resentment and anger can build, further depleting the tank, as you realize that the emotional energy needed to meet the demands of life is being "hijacked" by your partner, or given away in other ways because you don't fully accept and use your power to choose.

Many men don't realize the powers they're dealing with when it comes to their sexual selves, so they wind up making sexual choices that empty their reserve tanks. A man's penis is a marvelous and wondrous part of the masculine essence. It sets you apart from women, yet allows you to join with a woman. It's designed for pleasure, yet can be used to hurt, use and damage. Any man who seeks to experience his power to choose will be careful whom he touches with his penis. Condoms can't insulate you from the potential for pain your penis can get you into.

A man can get snared in the trap of thinking with his penis. Brains-in-your-underwear thinking results from misunderstanding sex. Sex isn't a game to be played. If you play at sex, your choices will diminish. Your sexuality is an avenue to deeper intimacy which can be shared between two people who care for one another.

In order to take charge of their reserve tanks, women must fully accept the fact that sexual expression is *not* a way to win a man. Often a woman believes that if she gives herself to a man sexually, he'll love her for it. If she's good enough in bed or if she shares herself freely enough and can please her partner well enough, she'll be able to hold on to him. He'll come to love her. This pattern sets her up to be hurt. Sexual expression that fills her tank must occur in a relationship that's already safe, secure and loving. Only then does the addition of a sexual connection between her and her partner make any sense.

The Power to Choose and Sexual Expression

A healthy sex life requires freedom to make choices. If you're to enjoy your sexual relationship, you must feel free to make a choice about what you'll do and when it will happen. If there's any hint of coercion, the reserve tank will be emptied a little. If your choice is surrendered often enough, the tank will be too empty for your sexual relationship to be satisfying.

Listen carefully. If your wife believes she can't refuse your sexual advances without penalty, her choice is already made for her. If your husband declines your sexual invitation, but is met with sighs, withdrawal or anger from you, he may give in to you in order to get along. If either of you—whether you're married or not—gives away your power to choose in this manner, you'll both lose something. You don't have to say yes. You'll need to take back your choices. Otherwise a healthy sexual relationship won't be possible.

When the power to choose is violated, the result in a woman is often called "low sexual desire" or "frigidity." In men common problems are "low sexual desire" and/or an inability to achieve or maintain an erection. Often focusing on reclaiming your power to choose is enough to restore more passionate sexual functioning if both partners are willing to work together.

In order to further illustrate this point, consider two examples. First, from a woman's point of view. Deena was sent to counseling by her husband, Sam, so "that counselor can figure out what your problem is!" Deena and Sam had been married for six years and had experienced ongoing tension with respect to their sexual relationship. They'd fought frequently about frequency. Her husband's most recent complaint was that she wasn't very responsive in their lovemaking. He also complained that she showed him little affection in the form of kisses and hugs.

Deena clearly stated that she, too, wanted things to be different. However, as she discussed the issue with me, it became clear that she'd allowed her freedom to choose to be violated. She wasn't exercising her power of choice. When her husband wanted intercourse, the only response he would accept from her was, "When, where and how many times?" In addition, kisses and hugs seemed always to lead to the bedroom.

If You Can't Say No You Can't Really Say Yes

The typical pattern Deena described went something like this. When her husband came home from work, he usually found her and gave her a kiss. Sam paid special attention to the passion of her kisses. If she kissed him with deep feeling, Sam assumed there would be a sexual encounter later. If she kissed him without much feeling, he would often withdraw. Deena wasn't always sure she would have any energy for a sexual encounter later since she'd been through a difficult day at the office and was now faced with dinner to fix, a house to clean and two children to care for. When her husband kissed her, she didn't return the kiss to any great degree because she didn't want to "lead him on," as he'd called it in the past. After the kiss he often would complain, "You never kiss me the way you did before we were married!"

This is where the power to choose comes into the picture. If Deena felt free to kiss Sam now with no promise of anything more intended for later, her kisses could be of a more passionate variety. Because she hadn't exercised her power to choose, she held back even on hugs and kisses. In this way she robbed both herself and her husband of closeness that would otherwise be possible.

In counseling we focused on her ability to set limits. She could kiss Sam enthusiastically without signing up for a sexual encounter later. At first her husband was angry that she would turn him down and stand by her choice. He continued to complain that she was "leading him on" when she kissed him warmly early in the evening, but later said she wasn't interested in intercourse. Deena stuck to her guns.

She also learned new ways to indicate to her husband what would be enjoyable for her when they had a sexual encounter. Sam was a little intimidated at first when Deena would say, "Rub me right there." Deena stayed with it and after a few weeks, Sam began to see the dividends of her reclaimed choices. Her tank began to fill. She experienced her power to choose. Deena even began to initiate an occasional sexual encounter, behavior that was very new for her. *Both* Deena *and* Sam benefited because Deena reclaimed her power to choose!

Consider a second example in which a man was thought of as the one with the problem. Ted and Linda decided to try counseling in order to deal with his difficulties with being unable to maintain an erection. Initially he'd been able to achieve an erection, but hadn't been able to sustain it long enough to climax. Lately he couldn't "get it up" at all.

It took only a few questions to confirm the problems he was experiencing were related to his eroded power to choose. He was violating the basic principles of his freedom of choice. Because he couldn't say no, he couldn't say yes.

Linda had decided that she wanted a baby, but Ted didn't agree that the timing was right for them to begin a family. They'd discussed starting their family a number of times. Ted had grown weary of the conflict and the last time they'd talked about it, he'd finally given in. Linda was elated, thinking they'd made a joint decision. She went off the pill and they were just going to "see what happened" as far as her getting pregnant was concerned.

Ted's problem with achieving an erection was the result of his surrender of his power to choose. He thought he couldn't say no to Linda about their having a baby, so his penis was saying no for him. His body was setting limits which he'd been unable to set in his communication with his wife. His failure to perform was a result of his relinquishing his choices. This was the issue we focused on in therapy.

Both partners have to have the freedom to say, "No." "Later." "Touch me right here, please." Mates need to have the freedom not to be in the mood. Only then can sexual involvement be as gratifying as possible. Paradoxically, experiencing the freedom to say, "I'm afraid I'm not really in the mood" may relieve the pressure and make it possible for "the mood" to be gotten into.

Men, Sex and Intimacy

Most men have a problem with being close—emotionally and physically. For instance, I've never had a husband complain that his wife has a problem with PDAs (Public Displays of Affection). I've never had a husband tell me, "Doc, she just won't hold my hand in public. And as we walked down by the lake at the park the other day, I attempted to kiss her and she just turned away!" I have had many women tell me something to this effect about their husbands.

Many men have been criticized by their wives because they turn over or get up and leave the bed after they climax. Their wives may describe such lovers as "rude," "thoughtless" or "selfish." The truth is, they're probably scared. Your lover may be afraid to be so close after being so vulnerable. It's common for a man to fear losing himself when he's in a relationship with a woman, and that fear is never stronger than when he's been especially vulnerable.

Men who experience the power of reclaiming their choices can be powerful, nurturing lovers. When you're confident and know you can maintain your boundaries, you can be close to your partner without fearing you'll lose yourself.

Men, Women and Frequency

It takes a tremendous amount of emotional energy to maintain a frequent and passionate sex life. You can't spend 12 hours of your day working, ignore your partner's needs, withdraw from meaningful communication and distance yourself from this significant person in your life and have much of a sexual sharing when bedtime comes. To do so is to fail to put gas in the tank and oil in the engine, then drive your car in a frenzy and expect it to last.

Come to think of it, many men and women neglect their partners the way they neglect their cars. They don't lubricate her regularly. They put gas in only when his tank is empty. They never touch him lovingly. They leave her parked in the cold and then expect her to perform to their wishes with the turn of a switch!

You need to know that if you want a frequent, passion-filled sexual experience with your partner, you'll have to make daily investments in the intimacy of the relationship. You can't have the result without a willingness to pay the price. Some of the things you'll need to focus on in order to fuel your sex life are—

- Consistent communication that brings you closer.
- Enhancing your ability to resolve conflict so that resentment doesn't build between the two of you.
- Giving your partner the freedom to say no without any punishment from you.
- Touches, hugs and kisses that don't necessarily lead to the bedroom.
- Cultivating a gentleness in your relationship that makes your partner feel respected.

Blockages in the Lines

When you've been the victim of any kind of sexual trauma, you may experience a blockage in the flow of energy through your sexual outlet. This blockage may be so severe as to completely prohibit sexual expression. It looks like this:

Sex Is More Than Body Parts

Blockages inhibit sexual expression.

When there's such a hindrance to the free-flow of emotional energy, unrestricted sexual expression isn't possible. You must first deal with the blockage before sexual feelings can flow freely.

The most common reason for the presence of an obstruction is sexual abuse. When you've been abused, the trauma will affect your current sexual feelings, thoughts and behavior. You'll need to have a patient mate in order to have the support necessary to resolve the abuse issues. (For more information on healing the wounds of abuse, see Chapter 12.)

Unresolved abuse issues will affect your perception of having choices. You'll relinquish your power to choose if you're still reacting to your mistreatment. Sexual abuse is a violation of your very personhood. It's a gross intrusion on your boundaries. If such issues are to be resolved and your choices returned, there will be much work for you to do.

Abuse takes away choices by keeping you stuck in the past. Options that might otherwise be open to you won't be explored because you'll be reacting to the molestation. Your response could be at either end of the spectrum. Often a person will be hypersensitive to his or her sexual self, acting on sexual impulses in ways that are compulsive and perhaps dangerous. He or she may pick up available partners who aren't really known and whose sexual histories may be sordid. At the other extreme, men and women may shut down their sexual selves, avoiding the stirrings of their sexuality in an attempt to detach from the pain of the past. Either of these answers will negatively affect your power to choose.

Fred's wife, Susan, had been sexually abused. She didn't know it at the time, but that abuse was at the core of sexual problems she was having with Fred. The issue which brought them to therapy was that she was experiencing a great deal of physical pain whenever they attempted intercourse. She'd endured the hurt over the years for the sake of her marriage, but after ten years of agony, she was more than ready for a change.

She'd been to several doctors for physical examinations. She'd hoped that one of them could find some physiological explanation for her pain. All the examinations had indicated that her problem had no organic cause. She reported the sexual abuse in our first session, but didn't see how it could be related to her current problems. I asked her if she would be willing to explore possible connections between her abuse and the sexual issues she'd experienced. She said she was willing to do so.

I asked Fred for his patience as I worked alone with Susan. He was supportive, although he had his days of frustration. With his encouragement, Susan and I worked together to unravel her story.

The perpetrator had been her older sister's husband. When she was a teenager, he'd abused her in her parents' home. A common scenario would involve his being asked by Susan's parents to help her with her homework. They would be dispatched to the table in the kitchen. While they worked at the table, he would fondle her. Her way of dealing with the pain of this violation was to withdraw from herself, to separate herself from what was happening.

There were also times when he'd come by the house when her parents weren't at home. Mom and dad worked on Saturdays, so she was left alone. Her brother-in-law knew that she would be by herself. He would stop by the house, letting himself in and quietly creeping toward Susan's room. She could hear him walking down the hall, then hear her doorknob rattle. She'd cringe in fear, praying that she'd remembered to lock the door. He never came into her room, but she lived in fear that one day he would.

When she came to see me, Susan was still withdrawing from herself and her sexual feelings. Cringing and living in fear were current responses she experienced in her sexual encounters with her husband. These reactions prohibited her from relaxing, so she couldn't allow her husband to enter her without pain. Her arousal cycle was also blocked by the unresolved molestation.

Susan had many negative messages about sex which we explored. She perceived sex as something men *did* to women. It was base and animalistic. However, if a woman wanted to keep a man, she had to suffer through sex. Women couldn't be expected to enjoy their sexual relationship. This view of sex robbed her of her choices. Her sexual self-concept needed to be changed if the couple's sexual relationship was to improve.

An important step in resolving past abuse is breaking the silence. A common saying in recovery work is, "You're only as sick as your secrets!" The silence was broken when she told me about what had happened. Susan also told her mother, whom she found to be supportive and very concerned. Her sister had long since divorced her husband, so she chose not to tell her sister.

Fred and Susan were very different in height and size. She was small and petite, while he was tall and wide. This difference in their sizes created an additional problem for Susan because she felt overwhelmed by her husband when they were in bed together. The traditional missionary position was especially threatening to her. They experimented with other positions, especially those which would put her in charge of the initiation of penetration. They found that with her on top, she felt safer. They completed a series of exercises which allowed her to dictate the speed and progress of their sexual encounters. Since she was on top, Susan could control the pace of foreplay and the depth of penetration. This feeling of personal power allowed her to be more responsive to her husband. She was able to experience the return of her power of choice.

The dividend for Fred was sizable. Susan became a much more willing and involved sexual partner. It was necessary for him to be patient and supportive for them to be able to get to that point. She needed freedom to exercise her choices. Because Fred was willing to give her the space to work on her abuse, she was finally able to more freely say, "Yes!" to him.

As you saw in Chapter 13, men also struggle with sexual expression when they have been the victim of abuse. The story of Nate, which opened that chapter, illustrates the ways in which abuse inhibits choice. He'd been sexually abused by a scout leader when he was eleven. His abuse was like a leash that allowed him to go only so far before hitting a limit that jarred him back into a limited area of his life. He was giving up choices because he hadn't resolved his violation.

As Nate worked through his abuse, he realized two major benefits which directly affected his sexual relationship with his wife. First, he released a lot of ever-present, low-grade anger. This had kept him at a distance from his spouse and had interfered with their intimacy. Second, he could allow himself to be more vulnerable with his wife. Before he began his work, he would go to sleep very quickly after sexual relations. Now he found himself wanting to talk, hold and be held afterwards. This time of bonding after their sexual encounters helped fill their tanks and draw them closer as a couple.

PLISSIT: Categorizing Issues

Counselors use an acronym to assess the intensity of a client's sexual concerns. The word we use is "PLISSIT" and it stands for:

P   =   Permission
LI   =   Limited Information
SS   =   Simple Suggestion
IT   =   Intensive Therapy

Often permission is all that's needed for you to restore your sense of personal power. I once saw a minister who was friendly and talkative, but who seemed to have a difficult time getting to his real problem. We talked about a number of issues which seemed to be only minor concerns. Well into the session, he finally stated the concern that had moved him to make an appointment. He and his wife had been engaging in a sexual practice he was unsure about. One night after their ten-week-old nursing baby went to sleep, the two of them were playing around in bed. As a part of foreplay, he'd sucked on one of his wife's breasts, receiving a squirt of milk. They'd both found this pleasurable and had continued the practice in later love-making sessions. He wanted to know if there was anything wrong or perverted in what they were doing.

This isn't a question they teach you the answer to in graduate school. I thought quickly and asked, "Your wife enjoys this part of your love-making too?" He assured me that she did. "And the baby is getting enough milk?" Again he said yes. I told him that I could see no problem with what they were doing, he paid his fee, and I never say him again. He just needed an "expert" to give him permission.

Limited Information is any information that will enhance the sexual experience. Explaining the location of key body parts and describing the difference in the arousal cycle of the male and female are examples of such information. Understanding the differences in what's exciting to the opposite sex in general and your partner in particular and how that differs from what arouses you is also an example of important information which can enhance your sexual experience.

Simple Suggestions are directives that lead toward more rewarding sexual expression. "Why not use a lubricating jelly?" "What would happen if you started with a back rub?" There are a series of exercises called "Sensate Focus" which guide couples on a gentle journey of rediscovery of the value of intimate touch in a no pressure atmosphere. I have often suggested these for couples with a sluggish sex life.

Intensive Therapy is often required for couples with sexual issues. Whenever a couple tells me that they have an issue that's strictly sexual, I usually say to myself, "We'll see." As several of the examples in this chapter illustrate, many sexual concerns grow out of problems in other areas which impact the sexual relationship. Unexpressed resentments, inability to communicate effectively, giving up your choices, trust and control issues and past sexual abuse are examples of common problems which can lead to sexual issues.

POWER TO CHOOSE: Use the following questions to do a self-assessment of your sexual self-concept and of your sexual relationship:

What's the current level in your reserve tank? Is it high enough to allow sexual energy to flow freely from your tank?

_____

_____

What do you perceive to be the current level in your partner's reserve tank? Is it high enough to allow sexual energy to flow freely from his or her tank?

_____

_____

Have you allowed yourself to feel the power of your personal power to choose in your sexual relationship?

_____

_____

_____

If You Can't Say No You Can't Really Say Yes

Has your partner allowed himself or herself to feel the power of his or her personal power to choose in the sexual relationship with you? Remember: If you can't say no, you can't really say yes.

_____

_____

Is there any unresolved trauma which blocks the free expression of sexuality for you or your partner?

_____

_____

Are you willing to invest the time and energy necessary to build intimacy in your relationship?

_____

_____

_____

If you're willing to do the work, a more satisfying sexual experience awaits you. With a willing partner, there's no limit to what you can accomplish!

16

WHAT'S WRONG WITH US?
Problem-Solving When Relationships Don't Improve

EVEN WITH THEIR BEST EFFORTS, some couples find that their relationships don't improve when they learn to reclaim their power to choose. Some couples, or at least some individuals who are a part of a couple, do their best to enhance their lives and their relationships, only to flounder, suffer, and often, break up or divorce.

What is it that separates successful couples from those who are unsuccessful when it comes to enhancing their partnerships? Often it seems that there are as many answers to the question as there are couples who are posing it. However, there do seem to be several themes or issues that come up repeatedly that keep some couples stuck. It's my hope that discussing some of these issues may help you problem-solve in your own situation and find answers to improving your relationship through reclaiming your power of choice.

Inability to Negotiate Independence

Remember that one of the cornerstones of experiencing your personal power to choose is the ability to freely choose what you want. This involves being able and willing to feel your own feelings, taking responsibility for your own life and choices and allowing the other people in your world to do the same. Some people find this difficult to do. Many women are afraid to set a limit for fear the another person might object. Some men never really get around to asking for what they want. Other people are too enmeshed with their partner to ask for or allow independence.

An inability to negotiate independence inhibited the progress of Harold and Dusty as they attempted to improve their relationship. Dusty had grown up in an alcoholic family. Even though her dad stopped drinking when she was seven and remained sober the rest of his life, the family continued to be troubled by the effects of his years of abuse. She was haunted by the memory of his angry outbursts. As a child, she would lie in her bed, terrified that the belligerent, verbal abuse that her mom was receiving in the next room would soon be visited on her. She feared her mom would be killed or leave, deserting her to live alone with dad. The sense of fear and abandonment she felt gripped her. Thirty-five years later those memories still troubled her.

Harold and Dusty married when he was 23 and she was 19. Harold had been her source of security since they'd begun their relationship. For many years he felt good about being needed by his wife. She seemed to lean on him and depend on him as her source of support and stability. Dusty both appreciated and resented him for the strong influence he'd exerted over her life.

After twenty years of marriage, Harold began to resent Dusty's push for closeness. When he began to work toward change, he didn't ask for the independence he wanted from her. Instead, he pulled away from her. For years he'd done everything she'd wanted. They bought what she wanted, moved into larger homes, and spent most of their evenings together. Over the years his tank became more and more empty. When Harold began to pull away in order to protect the little emotional reserve he had left, Dusty responded by pushing even harder for closeness. Since she didn't understand what he needed, her reaction made things worse. The more she pushed for closeness, the more Harold withdrew. Soon they'd established an ever increasing pattern of her pursuing and his withdrawing. Feeling he couldn't take any more, Harold moved out.

As they tried to focus on making changes in their pattern of marriage, their inability to separate emotionally from one another made it impossible to make any significant progress. Harold continued to take care of Dusty by doing things he knew she'd come to expect. She was frantic for his attention, expecting him to hold, hug and kiss her with passion each time they were together. Eventually Dusty was able to take some positive steps toward greater independence, but Harold found it difficult to let go of the care-taking role he'd adopted over the years. Even though he said he wanted change, he was unable to deal with the loneliness of life without someone to take care of. Because they couldn't detach and find a greater level of independence, his attempts to regain his choices were thwarted.

Following Old Rules Which Limit Growth

Leo is stuck in the past. He's following some old rules which are making it difficult for him to find new ways to fill his tank and to limit what goes out. These old guidelines have the effect of setting the valves on the tank at some predetermined level. Even with the work he's doing, he still feels empty because too much is going out and too little is flowing into his tank.

He sat down to examine some of his rules. He found some that he didn't even believe any more, but which he continued to follow. His list looked like this.

1. Be nice. Don't ever say anything negative to anyone.

2. Don't let people really know how you feel.

3. You can't trust people. They'll eventually hurt you.

4. Make sure everyone else gets what they want first.

5. Anger is dangerous, hurtful to others and ungodly. Avoid it at all costs.

6. Don't ask for what you want. People should just know and give it to you.

Leo was limiting himself by follow such old rules. He began to make more progress in his efforts to grow when he let go of or altered rules like these which limited his ability to make healthy choices.

Fear of Harm or Loss

Herb's boss is more than authoritarian, he's just plain mean! He'll criticize his employees in abusive terms in front of other employees. His basic guideline for management seems to be, "What the hell's wrong with you and don't you feel just horrible about it?"

He caught Herb the other day and really blasted him over a mistake in some paper work that wasn't even Herb's responsibility. Herb thought, "I've had enough of this. I'll just walk out! No one would blame me if I were to quit!" But then he thought about his mortgage and his car payments and credit card bills. He imagined telling his wife, "Honey, I quit my job today!" He decided that he had to stay. "I hate it here, but I have no choice!" he thought.

Remember, there are always choices. You may feel trapped, but you aren't. While you don't walk out of a job without thinking it through and you definitely don't walk out every time there's a problem or you and your boss disagree, you can leave a work setting that's damaging to your reserve tank. The damage may be caused by abusive criticism, a shaming management style, unrealistic expectations for production goals or outrageous demands for hours worked. You can set limits. You can say, "No!"

It's true that you may not be able to say no and stay in this job. The possibility of leaving will have to be considered, whether your leaving is by your choice or your employer's choice. However, since you live in a world of plenty where there's always enough to go around, there will be another job for you. You'll have other possibilities.

Failure to Maintain Changes Made

Mattie and Richard came to counseling at his encouragement. She said she wanted a separation and possibly a divorce because they'd both been very unhappy for a long time. She was doubtful that things could change enough to convince her that the marriage could be more satisfying. As counseling progressed, enough changes occurred that she changed her mind and reinvested herself in their relationship. However, when the changes that had been made weren't maintained, she eventually went through with the divorce.

For Mattie, the biggest issue was that she didn't feel important to her husband. His work, his family and his friends all seemed to have a more prominent place in his life than did she. She didn't just feel like a second banana, but more like a fourth.

They didn't talk about important things during the course of their 12 year marriage. They both had a very hesitant style of communicating that dictated that they couldn't ask directly for what they wanted. She saw that Richard's outside activities were infringing on the closeness that could have been theirs, but she avoided talking about it. She said that she didn't want to put pressure on her husband. Instead, she suffered in silence as she watched the other people and activities in his life pull him away.

As they started counseling, Mattie was still hesitant to ask for what she wanted. However, at the counselor's request, she made a list of needs, boundaries and consequences. She specifically asked Richard to spend more time at home. She told him that she felt frustrated because she'd watched them become married singles. She wanted more time with Richard, time that could be spent walking, talking, and in general sharing more of life together.

Richard responded positively to her requests. He began coming home earlier. He limited his time with his family. He went out with friends less and with Mattie more. They even found themselves turning off the television and playing a game or having a long talk.

As things began to change, Richard and Mattie quit coming to counseling. Thinking she had what she wanted, she didn't push for more time in sessions. Their counselor called to express his concern at stopping so soon, but she said that things were going great and they didn't return for some time.

Eight months later Mattie appeared for a session to say that she'd decided to file for divorce. When the counselor asked what had happened to lead her to this decision, she reported that the initial changes hadn't been maintained. She'd allowed her boundaries to be violated again as Richard began working late at the office and became over-involved with his family. She even watched as Richard said he had to let his alcoholic father move in with them. His father been long since divorced from his mother and "had no place to stay." While he stayed with them, he paid no rent, borrowed money he didn't repay and ran up sizable long distance telephone bills. By the time Richard's father had been with them for three months, Mattie had lost all desire to make things work.

Remember that things must change at some point if a marriage is to improve. However, if the changes are only temporary, if they aren't maintained, frustration and empty tanks will once again return.

Too Much Scar Tissue

By the time a person or couple gets to the counseling office of a helping professional to talk about their relationship, it's not uncommon for there to be some amount of resentment or bitterness present for one or both partners. These feelings act as barriers to healing. Like scar tissue in the human body, these wounded places can inhibit healing and lead to prolonged pain. The wounds may have been noisily inflicted, as when there have been loud and animated arguments, or they may have been silently imposed by years of unmet needs. Either way, there may be so much damage that little can be done to reverse its effects.

When Diane started counseling, she told horror stories of her last eight years with her husband. Things had gotten so bad that she'd divorced him three years before. A few months later, he'd been able to talk her into marrying him again. He made sincere-sounding promises of change. However, very quickly it became apparent to her that his change hadn't been sincere and that she was ready to get out.

Her husband asked to meet with me and this was arranged with her permission. He took responsibility for his part of the problem and admitted that he hadn't been the person or the husband he needed to be. I asked him why he was interested in working now, after so long a delay. He replied that for the first time he saw clearly what he stood to lose.

I referred him to a fellow counselor who worked with him for several months. The other therapist indicated to me that the work the husband was doing seemed sincere. However, when I talked to Diane about what was happening, she said she just couldn't bring herself to try again. She'd been disappointed too many times. There'd been too many wounds. She wasn't willing to open herself up again to the possibility of experiencing further pain. There was too much scar tissue.

Haven't Yet Been Honest

In order for lasting change to occur, both people in a relationship have to be honest about how they feel, what they want and how they've been disappointed or hurt. Without such genuineness, effective change won't occur. Areas have to be explored and altered after an honest inventory has been taken. If this frankness hasn't been shared, the absence of an honest inventory of your needs sets up the continued emptying of your tank.

The presenting problem for Tad was his depression and frequent anxiety attacks. When he appeared for counseling, he looked drawn and tired, like a person who'd worked many days without sufficient sleep. He talked in a monotone about his frustration with his job. He didn't find it fulfilling or challenging. He also mentioned some ongoing tension with his parents and struggles with his religious beliefs. These two issues were highly connected in his life, since his dad had been and presently was a minister. Initially, he didn't mention anything about problems with his marriage. In fact, he assured me in our initial sessions that things were great at home.

Tad's usual way of dealing with his sad thoughts was to push them away. He was afraid that if he allowed himself to relax at all, he'd get really down. Consequently, he worked very hard not to be depressed. The result was that he'd never learned much from his feelings of depression. The unmet needs of his life that had led to the depression he so carefully avoided were left unexplored. Explaining how essential it was for him to listen to his feelings of depression, I gave him his first assignment: spend twenty minutes a day investigating your depression.

At his next session, Tad came in with a list of several things about which he was depressed. The list included issues about work, his relationship with his father and minor irritations in his world. At this point, his marriage still wasn't on the list. There seemed to be something more he needed to learn from his sad thoughts, so for the next two sessions, I encouraged him to go even deeper into himself in order to find other sources of his depression.

At our fifth meeting, Tad appeared less depressed. His voice had more inflection. He talked with more enthusiasm. It was obvious that there was something new or different going on with him. He told me that he'd finally found the greatest source of his depression. It was his marriage. He was unhappy and had been for a long time. When he admitted this to himself during the week, his depression had lifted significantly. Now he was experiencing a new feeling. He said that he was scared, afraid that his marriage might be over. That day in our session he said that the odds were pretty good that his marriage would end. He indicated that more than half of him was already out of the relationship.

I encouraged him to express his concerns to his wife. In our session, we discussed ways in which he might raise his issues with her. The next time we met, Tad proudly told me that he'd been able to tell his wife what troubled him about their relationship. He told her what he needed and suggested changes. "How did you find the courage to tell her these things, since you'd kept this to yourself or so many years?" I asked. His answer indicated that he'd taken two steps in order to be able to talk to his wife. First, he came to see that whether his marriage ended or continued, he could stand it either way. Second, he was finally very honest with his wife. He said, "I decided that I had nothing to lose. The marriage might be over anyway, so I went for broke. I shared all my concerns with her."

During all the years that Tad had been so unhappy, he'd imagined that if he were to be completely honest with his wife, she would pull further from him. "Talking about it would have only made it worse," he'd said. When he actually talked to her, he found instead that the genuineness he'd instigated made them closer. His willingness to open up the issues in their marriage for discussion allowed them to begin the process of focusing on what needed to be different. She indicated that she was willing to work with him in changing their marriage.

Things don't always go this well when a husband or wife is finally honest with his or her spouse. However, the truth remains that couples can't change what they won't admit there is a problem. They continue to do the same things over and over that are unfulfilling or hurtful. Resentments build, stacking up in a pile that soon completely separates the two partners. Your choices will be yours again and your tank can fill when you're ready to be honest with your spouse about what you want.

Damaged, Leaking Tank

If you've tried to take charge of your tank and your choices, but still haven't experienced an increase in the level of your reserve, it may be because you have a weak or damaged tank. No matter how well you do at limiting what goes out of and increasing what comes into your tank, if the tank itself is leaking, you'll still experience physical and emotional pain and have to contend with a low level in your reserve tank.

Recall that your tank can be damaged by abuse of any kind and/or not being nurtured by the big people in your world as you're growing up. If the walls of your tank are damaged, the tank will be unable to hold the energy you put inside of it. Like carrying a leaking bucket, you'll experience the frustration of putting energy in your tank, only to see it drip away from you!

You can't ignore the effects of a damaged tank without negative consequences. Unless you're willing to do the work necessary to heal the tank, you'll continue to lose energy.

Scott had done a great amount of work on himself. He'd recognized the wounds that had been caused by the quality of the parenting he'd received and had begun to heal these hurts. He'd seen the ways in which he'd let others take advantage of him when he hadn't set healthy boundaries. He was doing very well at setting limits with the people in his world. He'd become more careful to recognize that he had choices and was taking more responsibility for the outcomes he experienced in his life. Still, something was missing. There seemed to be some sort of blockage in the way.

Scott was very frustrated. "I should be further along than this!" he exclaimed. "I've been working on these issues for over a year, and some days it seems as if I haven't made any progress at all. What's going on with me?"

He needed to go deeper, but he didn't know where to turn. What he hadn't fully realized was the damage which had been done to his tank during his early years at home. Scott lived with a demanding, emotionally absent father who never gave him the approval he needed to feel confident about himself. The damage to his tank continued to cause Scott to be in severe pain. It also wasted much of the energy that he placed in the tank.

Scott had a tendency to attempt to resolve every problem in his life by thinking about it. What he needed to do was do some *feeling* about his continued frustration. When he let himself be still, he became more aware of the pain, the emptiness he felt inside. He said it felt like a void, like a black hole inside of him. He came to see that it was time to do some more work on healing the tank itself.

Conclusion

Not all relationships can be saved. Sometimes there has been so much damage done before a couple begins to work on their marriage or dating relationship that it isn't viable. Just as some people who are brought into the emergency room won't walk out, so many couples who hope to improve their union won't be able to find enough life in their connection with one another to keep their relationship alive.

However, many relationships can be improved. If each of you is ready to reclaim your choices, most relationships can be changed so that they are more tank-filling than tank-depleting. Use this chapter's checklist to guide you as you seek to make alterations in the relationship you're a part of now.

POWER TO CHOOSE: Which of the hindrances mentioned in this chapter are limiting your relationship(s)?

_____

_____

_____

How do you want to respond?

_____

_____

_____

17

I GAVE AT THE OFFICE
Balancing Work With the Rest of Life

LARRY CAME TO COUNSELING only after the ache of his chest pains had become unbearable. He'd been living in extreme discomfort for several months, but all the tests and x-rays had been negative. The doctors had diagnosed his pain as being the result of "panic attacks."

His counseling began by taking an inventory of the stressors in his life. One of the most taxing was his work stress. He'd been in upper management in a food services company for 15 years. For the past five years, the company had been continually downsizing, asking the remaining employees to take on more and more responsibility while providing less and less help. Monthly quotas for the company required him to "bust his hump" in order to reach his goals. He was in daily contact with buyers, solving their complaints and negotiating with them for shelf space and special sales. Larry felt the squeeze from management on one side and his customers on the other. He compared it to being caught in a vise!

One of Larry's responsibilities was training the employees in his region. He conducted monthly training seminars which focused on sales techniques, product information, and company goals. It was his job to stand in front of the groups of fifty to two hundred and make his presentations. This was the setting in which he experienced his first panic attack. Even though he'd been doing these seminars for years and he felt confident that he could handle them efficiently, one day a voice inside told him that he wasn't going to be able to handle his presentation. He became nervous and agitated. His palms were sweaty and his breathing was difficult. Worst of all, his heart began to pound uncontrollably. Larry said it felt as if his heart was going to explode!

His description indicated that Larry's job was taking a tremendous toll on his emotional and physical health. The increasing work load he was shouldering coupled with his expectation that he perfectly perform his tasks were taking a tremendous toll on his tank. The amount of energy in his reserve tank was falling to progressively lower levels. Some days he wondered if he had the energy to handle all his responsibilities.

The tank falls to a low level if you can't say no.

My suggestion to Larry was that his body was attempting to set the limits that he had so far been unable to set with his words. He'd been unwilling to say, "Enough!" to his superiors. Finally, when his tank was nearing empty, his body took over to remind him that he was finite. His panic attacks were his body's way of saying, "This burden is becoming overwhelming! You can't keep this up and live!"

Larry had been unable to say no at work. Each time the company asked him to do more, he buckled down to do it. It was becoming increasingly difficult to keep up this pace. He needed to face his fear of not measuring up which hit him each time he stood before the men in his region to conduct a training seminar.

Reasons for Work

Why do you go to work? That may seem like a senseless question, but it's of the utmost importance for you to answer. Your response will indicate what it is that fills and depletes your tank. What gets you up and out of bed in the morning? What is it that pushes you or draws you to your office or place of business?

See if you can find yourself in the following reasons for going to work.

1. Dedication. You were hired or you began your business two or five or twenty years ago. You made a commitment to work and you're focused on keeping it. You wouldn't think of quitting or looking at other options. You haven't missed a day in ten years, except that one day when you got stitches because you cut your hand. If you're a working mother, you might stay home with a sick child, but never for yourself. You may be thought of around the office as a true "company man" (or woman), but you may be more dedicated to your work ethic than to the company itself.

2. Debt. You owe, therefore you work. A house, two cars, furniture and credit cards—you're in debt, perhaps even over your head. No matter how much you earn, it seems to take more to live. Since your obligations are at least staying constant and perhaps growing, it's essential that you work more hours if you and your family are to get ahead.

3. Definition. Your job defines you. Without it you would feel like less of a person. "I work, therefore I exist" is your credo. Even the *threat* of losing your job is enough to send you into a tailspin. (Historically, this has been thought of as more of a male point of view than a female way of thinking of work, but that stereotype is changing.)

4. Distraction. This is the classic case of the workaholic. Your work is used to numb; you work to stay busy because being busy allows you to distract yourself from the pain in your life. The hurt can take many forms—marital distress, sense of personal failure, original family distress. The ache is so intense that you can't let yourself relax for fear that you might actually feel it. Want a telling test of whether distraction is your reason for working? What do you do about work when you get tired? The true workaholic works *harder* when he or she is tired, rather than slowing down or resting.

5. Accomplishment. You work for the sense of pride and satisfaction a job well done brings you. You enjoy having goals and challenges before you. You don't have to have this job to feel good about yourself, but because you feel good about yourself, you do a good job.

6. Impact. You work because it's important to you to feel like you have something to give and you want to make an impact on your world. You're not so naive as to think that you can change the world, but you do believe you can leave the world a little better because you were here.

Where did you find yourself? Perhaps it takes more than one of these to indicate why you work. It may be that a combination of at least two or more of these more honestly describes where you are.

How do you feel about your answer? Are you content with your reasons for working? What changes would you care to make with respect to your attitude about your work?

Growing Sense of Disillusionment

Many people in our country are growing disillusioned with the American dream. The dream promises, "If you work hard enough for long enough and make enough, you'll accumulate enough to live the good life!" Many of you have given it your best shot, but found you couldn't find the promised result. Some of you have poured a sizable part of your time, and perhaps your soul, into a job. You may have enjoyed some financial rewards, but the end still feels empty. The promised outcome eludes you. The dream becomes an unfulfilled myth.

What's worse, in the hustle to make more or to accomplish more, many of you have neglected the other things that you say are important to you. Not the least of these are the relationships with your spouse, children and friends that you often sacrifice for your work. Many men get to the end of life and wonder, "I meant to be home more. I intended to spend more time with my wife and kids. Where did the years go?"

More women are choosing careers rather than jobs. They feel a need for a sense of satisfaction in their professional life that a job alone cannot provide. Yet many of these wives and mothers have a sense that while they find their careers important, there are other equally important responsibilities they are unable to meet in their marriages and their families.

Time passes so quickly. As you grow older, the cycle of life passes through birth, childhood, adolescence and adulthood with ever-increasing speed. Recently Max had an experience which drove this home for him. He and his son drove home with their families to visit Max's father. His son and his wife had recently had a baby and one purpose of the trip was to let grandpa visit with his great-grandson. As his father held the infant, Max was filled with a sense of wonder. Then the older gentleman spoke. He said, "Do you see this child?" He paused to let his son truly see their grandson. Then with a hint of a tear, his father said, "That's you yesterday!"

Time is flying by! Before you know it, your children will be grown and gone. They won't ask you to read them stories. They won't want to throw the ball around or shoot a game of hoops. If you don't take time for them now, when will you? How many hours are you spending away from your children and your spouse while you're at work. You'll need to ask yourself, "Is this career really worth what it's costing me?"

Many of you men learned to work by watching how your dads worked. You're imitating your father. Now you have the ulcers, the heart attacks and sleepless nights that he experienced. Sooner or later, the overwhelming schedule leads to burnout, an empty tank and fatigue. Whether your dad's living or already in the grave, you hope he approves of you as you work yourself into an early one.

Too large a number of women are working long hours at stressful jobs not because they've made the choice to do so, but because the family is in debt or they felt compelled by their husband or because a philosophy of equality they've adopted seems to demand it. None of these are approaches to working that will result in full reserve tanks.

Boundaries—The Road to Change

Many of you know you're burning the candle at both ends, but you don't believe your work habits can change. If you work less, you fear you either won't receive the financial or career rewards you want, your spouse will disapprove or your boss will be dissatisfied. Fear of losing your job may keep you stuck in a way of life that depletes your tank.

The illusion that you've been sold is that more work is better. The truth is that there's a point of diminishing returns. There comes a point when more work detracts rather than adds to what you can accomplish on the job. Consider the cycle of work and more work illustrated on the next page.

Your manager asks you to take on additional responsibility. He wants to hand over to you something "new" or "urgent." He may build you up to accept the job, saying or implying that you're the only one who can handle it.

At this point you know you need to say no. You're already frazzled or tired. Your tank is depleted. You have nothing extra to give. But you choose not to decline. You take on additional responsibility. You work longer hours and on weekends, hoping to be able to keep up.

At this point, several bad things can happen, all of which point out the damage done by this depleting cycle. The quality of your work falls. Your resentment toward your superior grows. You're tired, so you accomplish less. You work longer to do what you used to do in less time. You make more mistakes, necessitating more time spent in cleaning up your errors. Your creativity falls. You're tired and growing more so by the minute, but still you work harder.

If You Can't Say No You Can't Really Say Yes

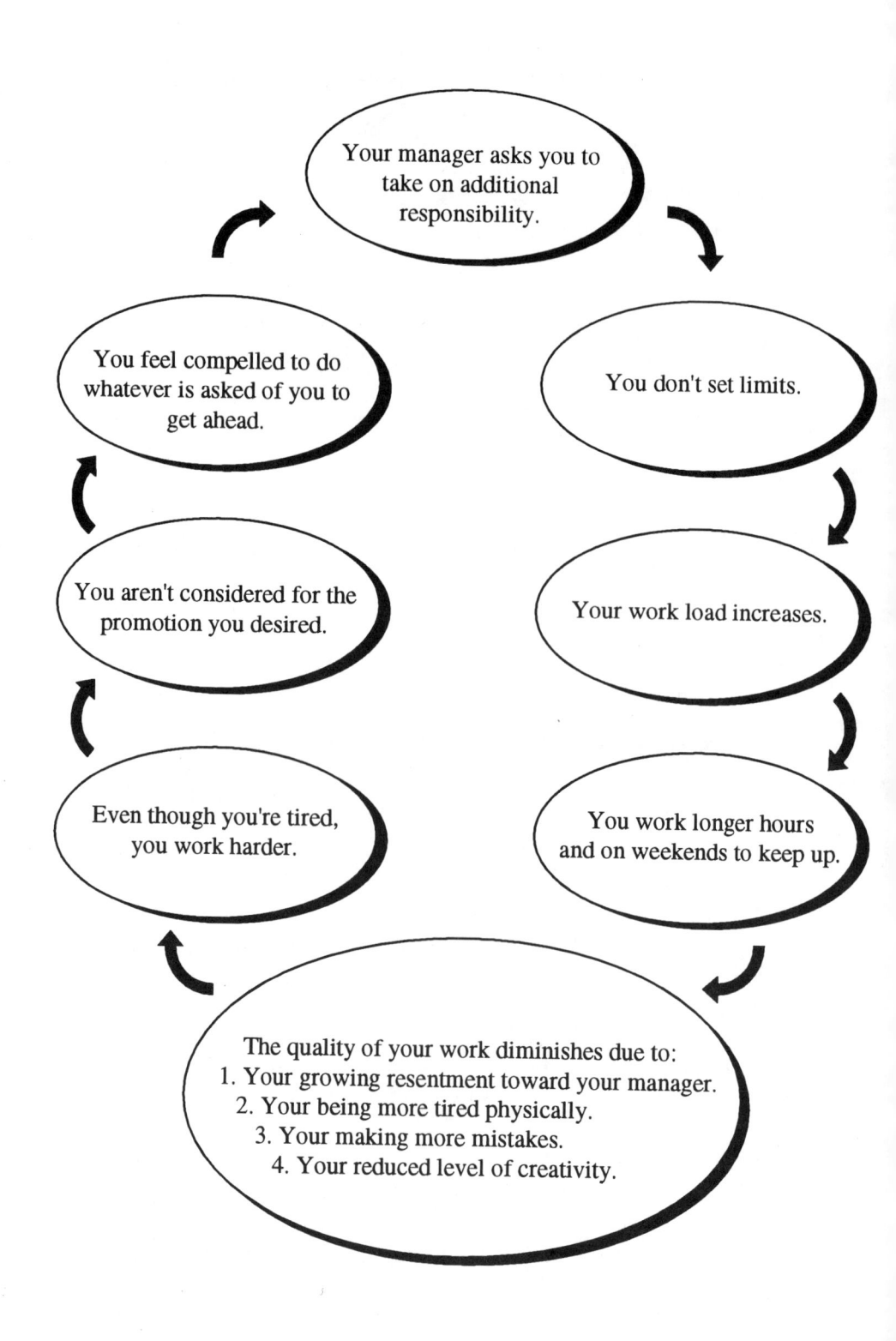

- Your manager asks you to take on additional responsibility.
- You don't set limits.
- Your work load increases.
- You work longer hours and on weekends to keep up.
- The quality of your work diminishes due to:
  1. Your growing resentment toward your manager.
  2. Your being more tired physically.
  3. Your making more mistakes.
  4. Your reduced level of creativity.
- Even though you're tired, you work harder.
- You aren't considered for the promotion you desired.
- You feel compelled to do whatever is asked of you to get ahead.

Because the quality of your work has fallen, you aren't considered for the promotion you'd desired. You have a renewed compulsion to do whatever is required of you so you can get ahead. And the cycle starts over.

Balance—Key to Success

It's hard to believe that getting ahead can happen in a much different way. There's another way to live. You can draw some lines to protect the store in your tank. You don't have to keep following the old, tank-depleting rules.

If you do nothing but work, you lose perspective. Your decision-making ability suffers if all you ever do is work. In order to be at your best, clear boundaries have to be set to protect your reserve.

This means you sometimes have to say no. Of course, if you want to move up, you'll have to be willing to work late occasionally, take on a weekend assignment, or travel. Those responses are part of being a team. But staying late night after night doesn't have to be part of your career plan.

How can you set limits without hamstringing yourself? It's essential to be direct with your boss while remaining flexible. You have to balance setting limits with being part of a cooperative workplace. Both elements are essential.

For example, in as few words as possible, you can indicate that regularly working on weekends isn't acceptable to you. You could explain that being balanced and having a family life outside the office are qualities that have made you the person your manager hired. It may sound impossible at first, but many executives have tried it and found that managers respect and value such firm directness.

Long explanations aren't necessary. If you have an obligation and choose not to stay for a late meeting, it's appropriate to say so with a minimum of detail. It's also appropriate to offer an alternative plan, like taking work home or coming in for an early meeting.

Remember that some work environments regularly require 12-hour workdays. It's essential for you to assess whether you can survive in such a setting. Few of you can, but some may be able to do so.

Henry did his job well for 31 years. He was the manager of a large computer department for an accounting firm. He was a dedicated and a hard-working employee. But he wasn't paying attention to the level of energy in his reserve tank. He pushed himself to work even when

If You Can't Say No You Can't Really Say Yes

he was ill. He'd only been out on sick leave four days in those thirty plus years. He was a teacher for classes at his local church. He and his wife raised three children, but he invested only a limited amount of time and energy in his relationship with his children. He was constantly occupied with something to do when he was home—working in the garage, watching television or sitting at his computer. It wasn't that he didn't love his family. He just didn't know how to stop working and he didn't know how to slow down and spend time with his kids.

One day after all those years on the job, Henry couldn't take it any more. He didn't know it at the time, but his reserve tank was empty. His supervisor found him weeping at his terminal. When he asked him what was wrong, Henry said he didn't really know. He just felt tired and worn out. He was having trouble holding it together. It was all he could do some mornings just to get to work. His supervisor was also a good friend. He suggested seeing someone he could talk to. He gave him the name of a counselor that had helped his daughter through the trauma of a divorce. The next day Henry made an appointment with the therapist and began the process of reclaiming his life.

POWER TO CHOOSE: Remember that the key to success in a healthy life is being able to balance making the money necessary to live on with other elements of a fulfilling life. These other elements include caring for yourself and building healthy relationships with other people. There are some important questions for you to ask yourself. If you're really ready for change, take some time to explore these now.

What's your overriding goal in life?

_____

_____

Are you balancing work and relationships in the way you would like? If yes, how? If not, what will you do about it?

_____

_____

How is what you're doing right now helping you reach your goals?

_____
_____
_____
_____

What will your quality of life be like five years from now if you're still doing this same job in the same way you are right now?

_____
_____
_____
_____

What physical symptoms of sickness and/or stress are you experiencing right now that are related to your work?

_____
_____
_____
_____

The situation can change! You can take back your personal power. Remember that your life's filled with choices. When you see and take responsibility for your current choices, you'll be able to make alternative choices.

A more balanced life is possible, but achieving it is up to you.

18

WHAT'S GOD GOT TO DO WITH IT?
Spirituality and Choices

FOUR WOMEN ARE SITTING in a doctor's waiting room. One of them is only there for a check up. She's had no symptoms and anticipates no problems. She's come in for her yearly physical. The second woman is healthy most of the time, but has been experiencing some mild pain in her stomach. She's here to see if the doctor can locate the problem. The third woman has been to the brink of death and back. She's been battling breast cancer, has had surgery and chemotherapy, and has been in remission for over four years. She never paid much attention to her diet before, but since her surgery, she's changed what she eats, omitting most of the fatty foods, sugar and the caffeine she used to consume. The fourth woman isn't doing well at all. She doesn't know it yet, but those headaches she's been having mean something very serious is wrong. Even with the best medical care, it's doubtful she'll be able to overcome this obstacle.

All four of these women have health. Some have good health, some have bad. One has better health than the others. One feels better than another. One is definitely in poor health. But they all have some kind of health.

I suggest this metaphor to you not to illustrate physical health, but spiritual well-being. You all have a certain level of spiritual health. Whether you're concerned about it or not, whether you care to explore it or not, it's there just the same. The condition of your spiritual self is very important to the condition of and level of energy in your reserve tank. It's important for you to stop and get a status report.

A Spiritual Core

If you wish to be a person who fully recognizes and responds to your choices, if you want to explore and live all of life, you'll have to rediscover your spirituality. Without a spiritual basis for your life, you'll die. Maybe you won't die physically, at least not today. But you'll die. Your emotions will shrivel up. Your life will seem pointless. Your choices will suffer.

Spirituality is the glue which holds your life together. It's your unchanging core, allowing the rest of your life to fluctuate while you stay the same. Your spirituality is your essence. If it lies undiscovered, a part of you is missing.

Royce is a man who has discovered his spirituality. In his men's group recently, he sat quietly, his face proud and somber. A hint of a smile was in the corner of his mouth. The men in the circle spoke one by one, catching the others up on what had happened in their week. Finally, it was his turn. He paused before he spoke. "God is gracious and faithful," he began. He looked each man in the eye, then he shared his testimony. "I'm ten years sober today. It's a miracle!"

Do you believe in miracles? Royce does. Not a raise-somebody-from-the-dead kind of miracle. The miracle Royce discovered was the life-giving essence of his spirituality.

Many women and men have discovered that miracles come from within. You can learn to expect a miracle in your life. This isn't the same as looking for magical solutions. Magic is looking for something "out there" to fix the part of you that hurts. Magic won't work. There aren't any special pills or mystic incantations. But there are miracles. Miracles not only work, they can transform your entire life.

Enhancing your spirituality makes a myriad of changes in the condition of your tank. First, it's integral to the healing of any holes in or damage to the tank itself. As you learned in Chapter 12, healing the tank is essential to having an adequate emotional reserve. Second, being aware of the spiritual allows you to perceive and respond to any number of tank fillers that you would be unaware of otherwise. For instance, the benefit of a quiet walk in the woods can be more clearly experienced when you understand how it can enhance your spirituality. Finally, a healthy spiritual self can help you maintain a higher level in your reserve tank by lessening the depleters that would usually lower your reserve. Consider that one of the most vicious emptiers for your tank is perfectionism. When you grow spiritually, you come to realize that being perfect is neither necessary nor advantageous for your life. When you accept this truth, your tank is no longer depleted by your mistakes and miscues.

Failure, falling short, making mistakes—it's all part of life. There's no question you'll fail if you're attempting to do anything of substance. The only question is, "How will you handle the failures?"

How will you respond when things don't go as you thought or planned? What will be your reaction to failed attempts to handle your world? The level of your spirituality is the barometer which dictates how you'll respond to your shortcomings.

Your spirituality will grow when you learn to accept more fully your humanness. To be human is to be imperfect. When you're stuck in your perfectionism, you're attempting to be God. When you accept your limitations and imperfections, you accept your humanity. This process is essential to a thriving spirituality. When you fully accept yourself as a human being, you release yourself from the burden of being God. What a relief!

Spirituality is much different than religion. Religion has to do with denominations and creeds and where you go to be with people of like faith. Spirituality has to do with the God-given creative energy within you. Your spiritual side is that part of you which empowers you to be all you have the potential to be. When you develop your spiritual self, you'll find creative powers beyond your mortal understanding.

One man who is growing said, "Religion is for people who are afraid of going to hell; spirituality is for those who have been there." That sense of wisdom that you often see in someone who has lived a long time and sorted out what is and isn't important grows out of the spiritual. When you've been hurt badly enough, you look for answers that transcend the material. Those types of answers are found in your spiritual self.

Royce, the man who is ten-years-sober, had spent years lost in a stupor brought on by drugs and alcohol. When work was too much, he used alcohol as a chemical to relieve the pressure. When there was conflict with his wife, he would escape. When the pain of his past, especially the memories of an abusive father, felt overwhelming, he checked out by smoking something, drinking something or snorting something. His tank was leaking like a sieve! He was in so much pain

Chemicals are often used to mask the pain.

that there was no way he could stop using on his own. He felt helpless to change his life.

It was then, when things were so bad, that Royce began to discover his miracle. He met a man who had walked the same path of pain and escape. He could identify with Royce and knew the anguish he felt. He introduced him to Alcoholics Anonymous, one place in our world where miracles happen. Royce's life took a new turn. A journey led by the spiritual began in his life.

Hindered Choices

Alcohol isn't the only form of escape from pain in our world. Some of you use television, food, nicotine, caffeine, sex, being in control or your work to run away from your inner turmoil. Only you can't ever do enough to escape being with yourself. The faster you run, the more tension you create. Soon, it takes more escapism to get away from yourself. Before you know it, you've lost your choices. You do it long enough and you begin to feel like you're not even in your life.

Developing your spiritual side gives you back choices. You'll be more honest with yourself and those in your world. A person who uses work or food or alcohol to cope with life loses touch with the essence of who he is. If he hides from himself long enough, he forgets the way home.

Paradoxically, your spirituality can give you back your choices by allowing you to see that you aren't in control. You try to believe some days that you are. Sometimes you wish you were. But the fact that you complain and fight and scratch and claw for what you want belies the fact that you're not in control. You know you're not. And you're not supposed to be. Your spiritual side grows as you accept that fact.

Attempting to be in control when you aren't is like doing your best to hold on to a wild stallion by means of a rope tied around his neck.

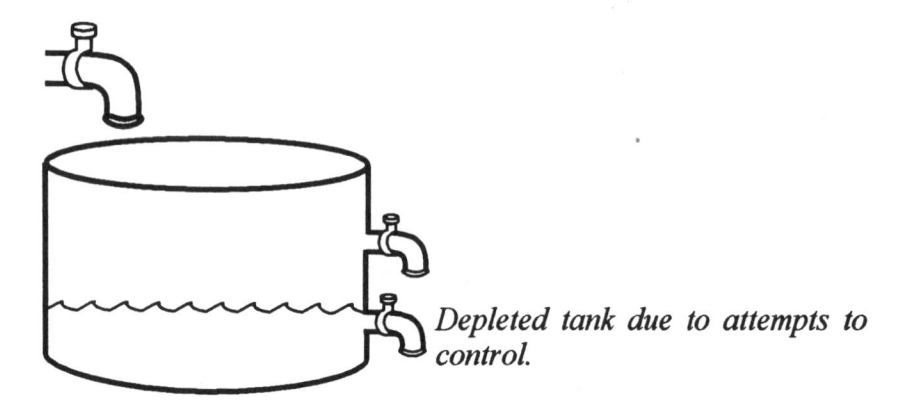

Depleted tank due to attempts to control.

You'll be pulled and dragged along, being beat up and wounded as you go. The way out of your pain? Let go!

Seeking to control what you can't empties your tank drastically. You'll be upset at what didn't happen that you thought should have happened. Connecting with your spiritual self allows you to let go. You don't have to control what others do or what they think of you.

Letting go allows you to be yourself. This gives you back your power to choose. You don't have to be what your boss or spouse or parents want you to be. You can be yourself. The more spiritual you grow, the more comfortable you feel with that. You learn that "you" isn't what you say or how you behave. It isn't even what you do for a living or what you own. "You" is who you are on the inside. Learning to honor and accept yourself is the challenge of the spiritual.

The way to grow spiritually is to let go. Nothing you could hang on to is worth more than your spiritual health. No relationship, no amount of money, no job—nothing is worth the cost if you have to sacrifice your spiritual self. And it's a lot easier on you than being dragged and pulled through life!

Free to heal and fill the tank.

With Awareness Comes Pain

Learning to live a life in tune with the spiritual doesn't mean having a life of ease. Pain is inevitable. No matter how much money you have, or how many people you have around you, or how much success you accumulate, you can still be hurt. Your spirituality won't protect you from the pain. It will show you a way of healing within the pain.

Opening up to your spiritual side isn't intended to be a new avenue for evading your difficult life choices or challenges. When choices return, there's often pain. Royce said he'd been free for ten years, but that wasn't a freedom to put on a frozen grin and ignore his problems. He was free to feel his hurt, anger, sadness and joy. He was free to be himself instead of what an ingested chemical made him. He was free to find a way to be in his life instead of running away from life.

Becoming Aware of Life

You'll have to stop and be still if you're serious about growing spiritually. A man constantly on the run can't be himself. Frenzy inhibits expression of your power to choose. Women who want to be whole must take time to stop and reflect. Time in silence may be difficult to find among the cacophony of sound you're exposed to, but it's absolutely essential to having a complete life.

Reclaiming your spiritual self means living in the present moment. Some of those moments aren't so good. In fact, some are downright overwhelming. While a healthy spirituality allows you the passion of watching a sunset in awe or being in a state of wonder at the birth of a child, it also allows you to feel deeply your feelings of anger, hurt and disgust.

Living your life aware of your spirituality is a more holistic way to live. You can see more clearly the interaction between mind, body and spirit. This allows you to live your life more as a connected whole. For example, the explanation of physical sickness in our country is predominantly a cause and effect model which focuses on symptoms. You have a headache? Take a pain reliever. You can't sleep? Take a sleep-inducing medication. You have a rash? Put a salve on it. Never mind that the headache was caused by tension brought on by mismanaged stress. Forget that the reason you can't sleep is because you're avoiding the painful reality of a deteriorating marriage. Discount the fact that your rash happens every time you eat a particular food and is likely a food allergy.

Things are changing. More doctors, dietitians and health professionals are stressing the interconnection between body, emotions and spirit. When you don't listen to your emotions, you blunder on in a clumsy fashion, like a horse in a garden patch. A lot of damage can be done in a short period of time. The more you push, the more problems you can cause for your physical and spiritual health.

Spirituality is a way of being. You may have seen the T-shirt that says, "I'm a human being, not a human doing." You need time and opportunity to "be" if you're going to find and cultivate your spiritual self.

You've got to spend time looking at the map. To be growing spiritually is to know yourself—thoughts, feelings and actions. You only know where you are when you know where you've been and where you want to go and where you are in that process. You have to pay attention to yourself like you pay attention to your driving when you travel by car. It takes effort to be able to do so. It takes time to "be!"

Challenging Your Religious Heritage

Many of you have resisted listening to your spiritual side because you have been so wounded by your religious heritage. A lot of you no longer attend church or synagogue. Others of you have gone back because you're still missing something you hope to find there.

According to a recent survey of baby boomers, two thirds of them dropped out of church or synagogue in their teens. Many of the boomers prefer to think of themselves as being spiritual rather than religious. Among those who dropped out, less than one in four have returned to active participation in a place of worship. While it's true that some churches and other places of worship can help you find your spiritual side, many more cannot. Some churches are more interested in enforcing a rigid set of rules than in helping their members find the creative energy that's present within each of them.

Your bad experiences with religion may have caused you to reject your spiritual side, too. You've thrown the baby out with the bath water. You need to know that you can develop your spirituality without experiencing again the pain you've had in the past from your religious group.

Wise Followers Who Set Limits

Your religious heritage may have taught you that thinking of yourself is wrong. All this talk about having choices and exercising your personal power to choose may go counter to what you were taught at your church. I don't believe there's any tension between what you've read in this book and what the Bible says about living a spiritual life.

As an example, consider one of Jesus' parables. Some of you who attended church or Sunday School as children probably heard a lesson on what's commonly called "The Parable of the Ten Virgins." The characters in the story are five wise and five foolish women. One reason the five wise virgins were wise was that they came prepared. They'd gone out to meet a wedding party. The group was delayed and when the bride and groom arrived, the oil in the women's lamps had burned up. The five wise women were able to refill their lamps because they'd brought extra oil. The five foolish hadn't prepared a reserve and so were left without oil.

The five women without oil said to the others, "Give us some of your oil for our lamps have gone out." The wise said no. They said that there wasn't enough oil "for both us and you." They suggested that those without oil go and buy from the merchants who sold it.

The wise women were aware of the amount of oil they had in reserve and could see that they didn't have enough for themselves and the others. They'd taken stock of the situation and knew the demands for oil and had made an assessment as to what their limits were in preparing to meet those demands.

In saying no, there's nothing to indicate that they were being spiteful. They simply placed the responsibility for meeting the need for oil back upon those who needed the oil.

Notice three things these wise women did:

1. They planned ahead by bringing a reserve of extra oil.

2. They were aware of how much oil they needed and how much oil they had.

3. They said no to the five who asked for oil even though they had oil and everyone could see it.

This parable emphasizes many of the points already made in this book. First, there's a need for you to be aware of your needs and your level of current reserve available to meet those needs. Being prepared implies taking inventory of your emotional energy and making a decision as to whether or not you have the resources to handle the situation. Further, those wise women were commended for their actions. While Jesus didn't specifically mention it, one of the things they did was say no. The story implies that it's okay to say no to someone who asks something from you even when you and they both can see that you have some of what they are asking for. Jesus praised those who set limits.

The Spiritual Advantage

Many men and women are finding that when you're in touch with your spiritual self, you recognize a new potential. You sense a renewed creativity. You find new and positive answers to the questions in your life. You get your choices back.

In the process, you can heal your wounded tank and stop the leaks that have steadily emptied its contents in the past. You'll recognize a new sense of life and energy that you never knew existed.

It's not easy, but it's a much more meaningful way to live.

POWER TO CHOOSE: What changes do you want to make in your spiritual life?

_____

_____

_____

_____

What do you need to do to make these changes happen?

_____

_____

_____

_____

AFTERWORD

On a clear, summer morning a young woman of eight was walking slowly down a long beach. She was completely absorbed in a self-appointed mission. Scores of starfish had been washed up on the shore when the tide had gone out. One by one she was picking them up and gently tossing them back into the sea.

An older gentleman who was a resident of the beach watched her from a distance. He eventually swaggered over and asked her what she was doing. The young lady replied very simply, "I'm attempting to save these starfish."

With a cynical tone, the older man remarked, "My dear, this beach is twelve miles long. You can't possibly get all the starfish back into the sea. You'll become tired or the sun will bake them before you're through." Then, as if to nail home his point, he added, "What you're doing can't possibly matter!"

The young woman tossed the next starfish into the ocean, and pausing only briefly, she said to the gentleman, "It mattered to that one!"

As a fellow human being, a speaker, and a therapist, my desire is to help others have a higher quality of life. Whether in my office with clients or speaking to an audience, I attempt to enrich the lives of those who've sought my services. One important aspect of that goal is helping men and women see that they have a tremendous power to choose. Every person has the potential to take charge of his reserve tank in a way he or she never has before.

This book is dedicated to that end. I have no magic to offer, only some words to share in pictures that I believe drive home the message. Not everyone is ready to listen, but some are. Some of you are ready to have more life. I hope this book is of some assistance in your quest.

After you've read this discussion and attempted to apply it, I'd like to hear from you. I'd like to know what worked for you and what didn't. Your story is of interest to me. Through such interaction, I hope to further refine the suggestions made here.